ANCHOR BOOKS

THE WAY IT IS

First published in Great Britain in 1994 by
ANCHOR BOOKS
1-2 Wainman Road, Woodston,
Peterborough, PE2 7BU

Foreword

Anchor Books is a small press, established in 1992, with the aim of promoting readable poetry to as wide an audience as possible.

We hope to establish an outlet for writers of poetry who may have struggled to see their work in print.

Following our request in the National Press, we were overwhelmed by the response. The poems presented here have been selected from many entries. Editing proved to be a difficult and daunting task and as the Editor, the final selection was mine.

The poems chosen represent a cross-section of styles and content. They have been sent from all over the country, written by young and old alike, united in the passion for writing poetry.

I trust this selection will delight and please the authors and all those who enjoy reading poetry.

Michelle Abbott
Editor

Contents

Unloved	Roy W Sayers	1
Colours	David J Cuthbertson	1
Weeds	Eugene Mehat	2
My Best Friend	Catherine Findlay	3
A Facilitator of Knowledge	Kathryn Marshall	4
The Angle Crew	Philip Gwyther	4
The Snow	Richard Page	5
Night	Joanna Rudge	6
Winter	Pearl Burch	7
Cometh the Snow	Patricia Haynes	7
Late Spring	Nikki Smallman	8
Lady Summer's Reign	Gloria Knight	9
A New Beginning	Christine Windridge	9
Birds in Winter	Lily Marsh	10
End of Summer	Joyce Green	10
Autumn Glory	Lilian France	11
The Ballet of the Trees	Irene May Smith	12
Trees	Leslie Smith	12
What is Nature?	Christine Jordan	13
Lily	Harry D Goddard	14
Dreamscape	Anne Franklin	15
Fickle Shines the Summer Sun	Keith Tomey	15
Gifts	Emma Jay	16
Winter Hardens	Jane Hanson	16
Autumn Months	David Rose	17
Happy Days	Olive Tilt	18
Summer 1993	Ronald Jones	18
War and Killing	Eve Chapman	19
Why?	Sheila M Stacey	19
Our Planet	A H Tonks	20
The Channel Tunnel	Joan Hubbard	20
A Tribute	Windsor Hopkins	21
Untitled	H Flint	22
Sacrewell	Andrew Byrne	23
By the Shore	Andrina Keeling	24

The Country Life	James Fleming	24
Lincolnshire	V M Goulding	25
A Birdseye View of East Anglia	Dora K Tack	26
Ballschadden	M McKenna	27
The Humber Bridge	Joyce Margaret Prescott	27
Night Sky	Sheila Grimwood	28
Homecoming	Sheila Goodman	29
War Widow	G A James	29
A Plea From the Heart	Derek Dean	30
Cry of the Hungry Child	Rodney George Priest	31
Greenpeace	Jenni Brown	32
Gulf War	Diane Hasler	33
Truth	Valerie A Preston	34
11th November	Rita Dicks	34
Ireland	D Iggulden	35
No More Wars	Alison Rumgay	35
An Inspiring Rain	Luke Palmer	36
Spring	O C Dunn	37
It's Spring Again	E Warren	38
Autumn Leaves	Norah Reeves	39
Bread and Childhood	Shirley Frances Winskill	39
Unsettled Mind	Terry Watson	40
Memories	Lily M Shipley	41
Life's Stock Market	C Chapman	42
Child's Play	Barbara Eastham	42
Every Day Blues	Lisa Marie Stott	43
Juggling Politicians	Peggy Moore	43
Bosnia	Felicity Robinson	44
Human Emotions	Dawn M Kingsbury	45
A Northern Ireland Dream	Victoria Sutton	45
Hiroshima	W Howes	46
A Tory Tale	Dot T Robinson	47
A Far Walk From Bosnia	Christine Makin	48

All Over Again	James Molineaux Starr	49
Six Days in June - 1967	Sylvia Lukeman	49
A Small Part in it all	Yvette M Ogden	50
Bosnia	Robin Lawson	51
Liberty	Shaun McDowell	52
Northern Ireland - Echoes of a Troubled Land	Jayne Marie Mottram	52
Lament From the Future	Betty Hand	53
Why	Lorraine Heath	54
Spiritual Wanderings	Sandra Glendenning	55
Flowers	Susan A Watson	56
Dawn Chorus	Leonora Steele	56
Farewell to Daylight	Pat Framton	57
All Kinds of Flowers	J Gowan	57
Winter Light	Helene M Verrall	58
Bright Star	Joan Deaves	59
Rain	Debbie Hayes	60
Autumn	S J Davies	61
Our Hedgehog	Leonard G Wordley	61
Summer	Valerie Deacon	62
The Fox	Evelyn Gladstone	63
Primrose	Eunice Cherry	63
My Feathered Friends	Margery English	64
The Storm	Mark Rogers	65
Our Garden	Muriel Richards	66
The Wonder of Spring	Olive Peever	67
Harvest Time	I Boyden	67
Autumn	Hazel Taylor	68
Autumn Glory	Doris L Middleditch	69
Summer Season	Maureen Rule	70
An Actor's Life for Me!	Brian J Singer	70
What if I	S J Flynn	71
Look Around	Leslie F Dukes	72
Feelings	C A Waldron	72
Love at First Sight	Brian Lawmon	73
Memories	Paul J Nabi	73

The Secret is Out	John D Mark	74
Things Happen to Me!	Kate Fell	75
Sarajevo Child	Joy Rowland	76
No Time	Liz Dicken	77
All Souls No Saints?	Raymond Dinsmore	77
Untitled	K Gordon	78
A Pray Time	Doreen Whall	79
Nightmare of Hypothesis	Soman Balan	79
Life in Exile	Frances Jones	80
Hiraeth (a Song for Welsh Expatriates)	R Evans	81
The Heart of Essex	G Wells	82
A Curlew's Cry	Michael Tod	82
Purley Then and Now	Maisie Dance	83
Imagine	Colin Cross	84
Imagine If . . .	Paul Corrigan	84
Armistice Day	Dave P Reddick	84
Remember	Edward Barber	85
War	Patricia Maynard	86
I Wonder Why	Irene Alder	86
The World Outside	Ann-Marie Lewis	87
Christmas	Mark Lewis	88
By the Sea	Alice Peterson	89
This Desperate City is Immortal	Olly Rees	89
Dreamland	C E Bradford	90
London	Paula C Graham	91
Our Land of Wales	Doug Stephens	92
Untitled	June Misson	93
The Secret Garden	E M Walker	93
My Garden	D J Hilton	94
Time is Winding Up	Colin Howard	95
We Could Save the Planet	Wendy Rowland	95
A Legacy to our Descendants	Jean Hopkinson	96
The Executive	Margaret Thompson	96

Blame	Jill McIlveen	97
The Six O'Clock News	G Saunders	97
Trouble Spots	Gill Sumner	98
The Day of Glory	Jennifer E Pocock	99
Deeds From Dreams	Robert James Carr	100
Oh I Hate Being Skinny	Ian Christopher	100
Imagine If	Gwen Albon	101
Imaginary World	Jean Carroll	102
A Double Life	Andrea Jane Biue	103
Eighteen Months Old	Sandra Coulter-Ellis	103
Clouds	Victor J Pike	104
Tree	Paul Lilley	105
Promise of Spring	Janet Endersby	106
Nature's Ways	John Whitwell	107
Autumn Leaves	Margaret Rose Marsh	108
Winter Seascape	Carole Smith	108
The Tree	Donna Payne	109
I Am the Golden Eagle	Lee Mitchelson	109
Through the Trees	H Smith	110
Late at Plough	Jim Hodson	111
Sunset	Matthew Longfoot	111
Graceful Waters	David Genney	112
The Leaves on the Trees	Brian Wood	112
November	J Brunskill	113
The Birds	Barbara Fleming	113
Old Age	A Cane	114
The Challenge	Thelma Robinson	114
Unspoken Words	Sheila Hutchinson	115
Mother in Law	Moyra Wells	115
The Dreamer	Esther Webster	116
Sarajevo	Sylvie Cox	117
Poverty	Lisa Kennett	118
Lock it Up	Evelyn Evans	118
Guns in Their Hand	Andrew Alison	119
Mugged	Alistair Miller	120
Scourge of the Skylines	Michael Woodhouse	120
Progress	C M Moody	121

The General's Accomplishment	Jassen Venkaya	122
A Ray of Hope	Lena Tavernor	123
Snow	Jerene R Irwin	123
Windy City	Eileen Ashbridge	124
Elegy	Joan Greathead	124
Kinderscout	Ethel M Stanton	125
The Stream	Muriel E Owen	126
Life in the 90's	Patricia Hepworth	127
The War Effort	Lesley A Baldwin	128

Unloved

A young mother's found dead
Her baby also, close by
Does anybody care?
Does anybody cry?

The little girl, just six months old
Starved to death, how sad
Mother tried her best for her
But it's hard without a dad.

Seven weeks they lay like that
No-one knocked or wondered why
They hadn't been seen for so long
Just forgotten, left to die.

Someone must have heard the baby screaming
But people now, say *I'm alright Jack*
And no amount of grieving
Will bring these poor wretches back.

All alone in her high rise flat
She lived to barely twenty-four years
Didn't anybody show concern?
Didn't anybody shed no tears?
Roy W Sayers

Colours

I ain't got time for singing the blues.
I'm too busy just keeping them back.
I have no time for a yellow streak.
Must be brave to find my track.
There's no money for a purple haze.
That kind of thing won't save my days.

1

I ain't got time for singing the blues.
I'm trying to mend my train of thought.
The train that's there steams black and grey,
And the fuel for fire is running short.
There's no time for seeing red,
Or in these tracks I'm left for dead.

I ain't got time for singing the blues.
I'll take the truth in black and white.
Green with envy holds no key.
Nothing's won from hate and spite.
I want the blue of a summer day.
Sun smile down your golden ray.

I ain't got time for singing the blues.
I'm seeking the cloud with the silver line.
My nails bleed in a dirty grey,
I'll work so hard till life is mine.
I'll see the red night, stop to think,
Believe my dreams and kiss the pink.
David J Cuthbertson

Weeds

The Scottish heights guarded the meandering road,
While the sun was melting the grey, celestial load,
Drying the green valley by drizzle humected.
Then, sudden miracle I had not expected,
The whole grass verge was gold! True, the gold was not real,
Thus avoiding the risk of anyone to steal!
Had it been the metal for which the world goes mad,
My friend, bank manager, would not have been so sad,
To see a man enthuse in front of weeds worthless.
Had they been daffodils, *mad your mind would be less.*

Oh! Wild flowers growing, not in a prim garden,
Not lovingly nurtured by the gardener's hand,
Men trample on your head which is of sunshine full,
And their only desire is from the soil to pull
That plant of all seasons that is only a weed
Which poisons their garden with its obnoxious seed!
Your head is beautiful: it has been made by God;
Your name given by men, to say the least, is odd.
Medicinal function in your body resides,
But when your radiant head in the landscape presides,
Fascinated I have, for admiring, to pause.

As I was thus musing on Nature and its cause,
A little Scottish boy by his shocked mother led,
shouted: *Mum, look! All gold, all golden Pee-the-bed!*

Spurned by the practical, the gracious flowers wild,
Had revealed their glory to simple little child.
Eugene Mehat

My Best Friend
You were my pal for nine long years,
You were by my side through laughter and tears,
Every one loved you my gentle giant,
To replace you I know that I just can't.
You made people smile, you were such a character,
With funny ways, that were unusual for an Irish Setter
Thank you Ryan for those wonderful years,
Without you life would have been hard to bear.
Your affection and memories I treasure
my bonnie lad,
You were the best friend I ever had.
Catherine Findlay

3

A Facilitator of Knowledge

A facilitator of knowledge is what I want to be.
So I'll battle through the elements, where units are the key.
I'll underpin my knowledge and gather up resources.
I'll identify and verify all components of such courses.

My performance criteria will be readily met.
My product evidence soundly set,
Range indicators will have reference,
Prominent theorists, given preference.

I'll jostle with the jargon and embrace abbreviations.
I'll accredit prior learning with the least of reservations.

I'll organise and summarise,
I'll supplement and specialise.
This is competence learning
and who am I to criticise?

And with my portfolio readily prepared,
verification will follow
and not a buzz word spared!
Kathryn Marshall

The Angle Crew

On storm tossed days white horses roam,
And biting winds gnaw every bone,
With cliffs and coves awash with foam,
Out go the Angle crew.
There's not a call unanswered goes,
The rocket's fired - they're on their toes.
The sudden fear that no-one shows
Will not deter these loyal few.

Through generations handed down,
When duty calls this tiny town
Sends forth their men of brave renown
To dangers on the sea.
A hamlet really - nothing more,
Right on the far south western shore.
But the crew is always to the fore
In its brave history.

A place of which most never guessed,
Who think of Tenby as far west.
But the splendour of this coastline blessed
Is a sight that all should see.
It can be dangerous and bleak,
In winter storms not for the weak,
Yet when summer days are at their peak
It's a magic place to be.

So if far west you travel down,
You'll maybe find this little town.
Its cheery face in summer gown,
Will charm and embrace you.
But try to get those memories told,
Of raging seas and sailors bold;
The legacies of men now old,
Of the Angle Lifeboat Crew.
Philip Gwyther

The Snow
Falling to smother all in my sight
Fall in my sleep one wintry night,
Fall while I dream of hot summer days
Bronzing my body in warm sunny rays.

Falling to cover all with your cloth
Fall to bleach clean this Earthly trough
Fall in wind directed wispy swirls
Creating images of heavenly angelic girls.

Falling to gravity's age old tune
Fall as aphrodisiac, the lonely swoon
Fall to be initiator of someone's fun
Turning off TV's and American guns.

Falling to see what you never have seen
Fall to be blackened by all that's unclean
Fall to a world that Nero would know
Fiddling to visions of a reddened glow.

Falling to see what virtues remain
Fall to be calmed by those termed *insane*
Fall to soon realise the madness beneath
Humanity's death is the cost of a wreath.

Falling to witness your purity's death
Fall to give weakness its last living breath
Fall in disdain of those on this globe
Who use all that's pure as an ugly robe.

You, the snowflakes, here on this land
I won't inherit, but 'tis where I stand
You give me hope of a better place
Beyond my reason, when all can be safe.
Richard Page

Night
Night is a black piece of sugar paper
in front of blue,
The stars are shining dresses
in the ballroom
doing the waltz.
The moon sits and rests on Mars.

Doors stamp and kick,
the letterbox mumbles
as the postman opens its tummy.
It hides under my bed
and feels the vibration
of me jumping up and down.
Joanna Rudge (10)

Winter

The stately trees are leafless,
The snow is falling fast,
An icy wind is blowing,
Winter is here at last.
Autumn has cast her pretty dress,
Now black and white we see,
Mothers draw the curtains,
Children clap their hands with glee.
We watch the snowflakes falling,
Clothing everywhere with white,
See the people hurrying homewards,
On this dark and gloomy night.
Home - however large - or small,
However rich - or poor,
Still they hurry onwards,
Till they reach their own front door.
Home - the place where we grumble,
Home - where the fires burn bright,
Home - sweet - sweet home,
Home for it's cold tonight.
Pearl Burch

Cometh the Snow

Now the snowflakes gently falling
Cover land and tree with white;
Reach cool fingers to the windows
In the grey and lilac light.

All the bushes in the garden
Bend liked burdened agèd men.
Every hill is like a mushroom.
Fairy trees grow in the glen.

Softly, softly fall the snowflakes
From the low and yellow sky.
Softly breathes the wind, then slumbers,
Muted is the owl's first cry.

Oh! what joy it is to waken
To a world of delight.
Every tree and hedge and garden
Hushed with wonder, awesome bright.
Patricia Haynes

Late Spring

Spring is the season
For young things to grow,
Lambs in the field
And no sign of snow.
Buds on the hedgerow
Everything green,
The weather's so beautiful
Not a cloud to be seen.
Children out playing,
In the warm spring air,
After the cold, cold winter
They haven't a care.
Everyone's happy now the
cold spell has gone,
The farmers are busy
For their work's just begun.
Nikki Smaliman (11)

Lady Summer's Reign

Welcome, Lady Summer and all the joys you bring;
Now buds of spring will blossom and birds will homeward wing.
Each busy little squirrel will seek its treasure store;
To reap the Golden Harvest of seasons gone before.
Your silky, golden fingers touch the trees in all their glory,
And speak to us, as if to say *old winter's had his story*.
Be gone, dark days and frosts that cling to every country lane,
For I am here to stay awhile - it's Lady Summer's Reign.
Gloria Knight

A New Beginning

A flower is in full bloom, the sun
is shining, the month is June. There
it stands head held high, looking
up towards the sky. There it blooms
all summer through, in evening light
and morning dew. But sadly
when the autumn arrives, that flower
bows its head and dies. All winter
through it's nowhere to be seen,
the ground is flat where that flower
had been. But sure enough when
the winter has gone, what
can I see in that morning sun.
Yes there it is with its head held high,
looking up towards the sky.
That same flower, it looks as if
it's singing, because it has
a new beginning.
Christine Windridge

9

Birds in Winter

Nuts in hanger, seed in tray
Sparrows never far away
Starlings land, strutting, squabbling
Crumbs and fat quickly gobbling,
Bluetits, garden acrobats
Blackbird warns of prowling cats
Collared doves call from the tree
Coo coo kuk repeatedly.
Dreaded magpie, black and white
Puts the other birds to flight
Robin comes when they have flown
He prefers to eat alone,
Watching, waiting, one regret
Haven't seen a song thrush yet.
Lily Marsh

End of Summer

Summertime is now on the wane,
Darkness descends too soon.
On peering through the window pane,
There shines the Harvest moon.

Pinks and carnations fill the air,
With colour and perfume.
A prudent time to stand and stare,
And hum a happy tune.

Berries forming, birds chirp with glee,
Trees now laden with fruit.
Late last night! Who did I see?
A hedgehog in pursuit.

He paused and thought, then hit the road,
Not sure of my intent.
So scurried off to his abode,
His mini garden tent.

10

High in a tree towards the park,
A cry is heard at night.
Upwards searching into the dark,
A barn owl soars in flight.

Wonders of nature are many,
Look for them every day,
For they cost you not one penny,
Enjoy them while you may.
Joyce Green

Autumn Glory

Autumn is here in her newest gown
Rich colours of russet, gold, red and brown
Leaves form a carpet in a golden haze
Morning mists and sunlit days
Raindrops glisten like polished glass
And lacy cobwebs cover the grass.

Squirrels are hunting in the trees
Bonfires are glowing
There's smoke in the breeze
Gather the fruits and store them away
Pick all the berries while you may
Just stop awhile, do not talk!
Hear twigs crackle as we walk
Look at all the changing scene
To autumn's brown from summer green.

Daylight is fading,
It's getting dark
Hurry home from the park
Draw the curtains and light the lamp
Shut out the cold and the evening damp
Tea by the fire, pull up a chair,
Summer had gone, autumn is here.
Lilian France

The Ballet of the Trees

As I look thru the window
On a windy day,
I see the trees all dancing
across the way,
tall poplars sway to and fro,
as if they hear the music come and go.

Bowing and waving
with such delight,
it surely is a wonderful sight.
A ballet in all its beautiful splendour,
is being performed for our blessed maker,
thanking him for their leaves so green
they truly make a wonderful scene.

But when the wind has ceased,
and the trees are at rest,
that's when you can see them
at their very best,
so tall and stately, full of majesty
just as God made them to be.
Irene May Smith

Trees

As I wander amongst the trees
I think to myself how it would have been
without these towering giants, now to be seen.
Their stretching branches and shimmering leaves
that float to the ground, making a covering
like an eiderdown of brown and green.

As autumn is here and the winds blow strong,
these trees bend and sway all day long.
Sometimes one hears a cracking sound,
then down a branch falls to the ground.

12

Oh, why is nature so cruel at times,
to do this thing is out of sublime.
but then this is how God created all things.

As we think and wonder why, of this destructive game,
and say, 'What a shame!'
It's all for a reason, to make new growth
and as these branches and leaves decay,
they feed the earth and keep it from withering away.

So now one knows, that all things are good,
to see these giants of trees, swaying and seething
to the ground,
it's for the likes of you and me,
to keep us earth bound.

Let's not forget the smaller trees,
their splendour is all to see,
as they look up to those bigger trees,
and think, 'Yes, *God also made me.*'
Leslie Smith

What is Nature?
I sit and ponder aimlessly
At the wonders of the world.
Bewilderment, astonishment,
Exceptance, acknowledgement;
Are the feelings that occur.

When nature's in her full attire
And blossoms all around,
The beauty that presents itself;
Can once again be found.

The sunrise in the morning.
The rain that makes things grow,
The birds, the bees, the flower, the trees,
Of these we all do know.

The sparrow in the garden
Singing in the tree.
The sparrow in the garden,
Who's afraid of you and me.

We put out little tasty bits
In the hope that he will find
All we want to do is feed him
And not to be unkind.

The buttercups in the meadow
Who raise their heads up to the sun.
Children laugh and giggle,
Life is so much fun.

As I sit there pondering,
I feel life is such a treat;
It gives us all the courage
For the adversities we meet.
Christine Jordan

Lily

Away, away, to the greenwood she races,
Out where the small robin chirps from his log,
Out where I go now in quickening paces,
Following the wake of my old collie dog.

There's a splash through the lonely white water,
In a forest of tall fern you hide,
By the aspen when tired steps doth falter,
I called and you rushed to my side.

Then together we stood in the still quiet light,
And her cold nose nuzzled my hand,
While watching old thrush gave voice out of sight,
As our homeward journey began.

14

For it is back to the homestead now Lily,
To our yellow brick house on the hill,
Where the clematis blue and the white roses too,
Are fair racing right up to the sill.

The old dog looked up her brown eyes intent,
Where those ceilings of leafage hang low,
Then via dingle via long hill, while slow our ascent,
I there with my collie dog go.

Through the old garden gate, now listing and worn,
On freshly rolled gravel we tread,
While far to the east saw the quiet breaking morn,
Where the sunrise had lit the sky red.
Harry D Goddard

Dreamscape
Water's shining bright in autumn sunlight,
Huge trees reaching around me;
Everything's such a beautiful sight.
Brightly coloured leaves twisting to a bed of rich soil,
Peaceful, quiet, still, humble and yet so royal.
This is the place I think of in my dreams,
A place of rest and tranquillity.
Anne Franklin (11)

Fickle Shines the Summer Sun
Fickle shines the summer sun on daisies in the field,
Peeled petals raised, Hosanna to blue skies:
A woman young, and love, soft amber skinned
Dark casts a shadow softly with her sighs,
As there she stoops and plucks one tender winged;
I love him - Oh I love him not, called oft'.
I look on and feel each painted petal torn
And tossed aside like paper dreams aloft;
Naked emotion - naked stem forlorn:
Storm clouds gather; fast fade the daisies in the field.
Keith Tomey

Gifts

Rain and wind, flowers and trees
Nature's gifts all are these,
Rain to make each flower grow,
Wind to howl and wind to blow.
Flowers for bees and flowers for pleasure
Trees to gaze on at my leisure
Leaves that change their colour
and fall,
from trees, some big, some small.
At my feet they lie in splendour,
red and brown and glowing amber,
and as through midst of them
I wend my way,
the darkness falls
and autumn makes another day.
Emma Jay

Winter Hardens

Melting dew disappear into a
hard frost, covering the grass
a harsh threat to the ground
along the hedges and fields
around A pale sky with a
slight shine from a hiding sun.
To the earth on the bare trees
where the cold now has just
begun.

An air of crisp coolness stretches
to widen the silvery whiteness of
a telling of the hardening of the
winter months to come. The birds
now quieten in sound but still a
soft whistle can be heard having
grasped to dread the expected hard
winter that lies ahead.

16

The sun shines more boldly as
the cool day lingers to chill.
A breeze tries to force through the
air but remains still.
The clouds do not foretell of a
snowfall but perhaps is yet to
come to the land, before the dark
days of winter draw to a close
till arrives spring and a new rose.
Jane Hanson

Autumn Months

Autumn wind blows leaves off trees,
Warmer days are overseas,
A time that is always cold,
Now the year is growing old,
Clouds are covering the sky,
And rain falls from way up high,
We are having longer nights,
Frosty air and conker fights.

Most leaves are crunchy and red,
Now summer is surely dead,
The frost is white,
Reflects the light,
In the wind the leaves will rustle,
Unnoticed by our daily bustle,
But the thing I like the best,
Is to have a rest,
From the heat of summer,
South all the birds are flying,
Now the year is dying.
David Rose (11)

Happy Days
Sweet bird of youth
Your flight is fast
Those golden years
Alas! Don't last.
Days that are sprinkled with
Sunlight and dew
A time full of laughter
Discovering anew.
Long golden days
Sweet precious hours
Why can't they remain
Like fresh morning showers?
Childlike we dream now
And capture so true
The feeling of youth
As each spring returns new.
Olive Tilt

Summer 1993
Springtime came and I saw it pass,
Then I waited for summer in vain.
I waited and waited forever it seemed,
But all it did was rain.

It rained, it poured, and more it rained,
I thought it never would lapse;
And it suddenly dawned on me one day,
That autumn had been and passed.

So a summer this year is not to be;
It is futile to wait anymore.
But there is one thing I know for certain,
Of a winter I can always be sure.
Ronald Jones

War and Killing

People say to me, *how would I sort it out?*
but I'm not that one who's claiming I can.
I just know that war's not the answer,
it only destroys man.
How can we justify killing?
One life is surely too much.
But they don't think of men, they think of figures.
I think they are out of touch.

Life is surely about living?
But greed and violence take its place
and rather than helping and giving,
we wipe out a whole damn race!

These weapons are made to destroy us,
the sword, then the gun, now the bomb.
How does anyone think they can help us,
when us and our world are gone?
Eve Chapman

Why?

Why in God's name is the world in such a
mess, thousands upon thousands of people
in distress.
Children cry for food. The old somewhere to
rest, why oh why dear lord can't you end
this bloody mess?
Come down from your heavens, so very far away,
Come soon oh lord, come soon before the
end is neigh.
Why oh why must all these people die?
Sheila M Stacey

Our Planet

Are we on a dying planet?
We must ask ourselves.
Are we on a dying planet?
A question that cannot be shelved,
with all these changes in
the weather.
We are all in this together
is it too late to stop a disaster
we all hope we can master,
Experts blame the ozone layer
it seems we are all to blame
through all mankind's misbehaviour
the future would never be the same.
What of our children's future,
our planet we must not destroy
we must do our duty and make the
future their joy.
With all the world's pollution,
can we hope to survive?
Can we find a solution?
Oh God let us hope and try.
A H Tonks

The Channel Tunnel

Whilst on holiday in Folkestone,
We went to an Exhibition Hall,
It's called the Euro Centre,
With information, which concerns us all.

They are building the Channel Tunnel,
Bored from rock, beneath the sea,
Consisting of three branches of control,
One freight, one cars, one emergency.

A massive construction, of concrete,
From Folkestone to Calais and France,
Fast moving traffic, will be in motion,
At a hundred and eighty an hour, they'll advance.

This Tunnel, was thought up many years ago,
In the days of shovels and picks,
When labourers toiled away their lives,
Now mechanical bores, do the tricks.

In a year's time, maybe a little more,
It will change our mode of life,
Some say it will be for the better,
Others say it will bring much strife.

Whenever you look in Folkestone,
Roadworks are all around,
With such a vast project underway
The countryside is chaos bound.

Maybe after completion, peace will return again
Nature will survive the turmoil and mess
Life will go on much as before,
For better or worse is anyone's guess?
Joan Hubbard

A Tribute
May I with use
of simple pen
pay a tribute
to Glamorgan.

Though others
pay a feality.
To Shires
which are unknown
to me.

I cannot speak
for other men.
Britannia has
my last amen.

Each man to his own
be true.
Let him in truth,
his duty do.

When my time comes,
to take my rest
to me; I will
have seen the best.

Forgive me:
if we don't agree.
But Glamorgan
is my home
you see.
Windsor Hopkins

Untitled
This lovely town of Melton
Astride the river *Eye*
Is famous for its Stilton
And also for pork pie.

It also boasts a couple of bands
Who've marched and played in many lands.

We've a swimming bath
That's second to none, a leisure centre too
And yet the young folk of the town
Still say *there's nothing to do!*

There's tennis courts and bowling greens
There's pitch and putt and putting
There's cricket pitches, football pitches
I'd hardly call that nothing.
H Flint

Sacrewell

Nestling birdlike between metropolis bound arteries
Lay a haven to bewitch all city slicker cynics
Its well pledging to replenish the shallowest soul
While the intense twig twiddlers douse for eternity
I weave through a minefield of decaying beet husks
Enticed by the watermill's ghostly yet resonant pulse
The gnarled wisteria trunk,survivor of human mischief
Shoots its warty tendrils to undermine yet further
The corroding mortar of the mildewed millhouse
Septuagenarian David retains his gravitational pull
A custodian of nature's spiritually enriched soil
Supervising, inspiring his loyal dreg tagged crew
To voluntary heroics no lonely epitaph could betray
His twelve saplings of Europe, unified in all respects
Bend double in flatland gales as their namesakes feud
What price the Gilbert collection? Dust and indecision
Eroding the sheen of this eccentric old fossil's vision
Mike Harding's slightly prettier twin collects gory faeces
From barn owls slightly less outgoing than Salman Rushdie
The neurotic bird scarer is on a commission only wage,
Yearning to trade his Accrington Stanley rattle for an AK47
They're dismantling Santa's Grotto and liberating his elves
As the supernova aconites herald the hosepipe bans of spring
The mangles and twin tubs ache for a sterile monochrome home
Free from the clammy prints of brats with trampoline sickness
To enable the media enslaved young to dissolve the tablet
Labelled *The Past,* the water must flow unmolested, unpolluted
If history is a bus depot, then Sacrewell is its Sunday service
Its only morbid sentinel a cardboard roman clad Roy Kinnear.
Andrew Byrne

By the Shore
Isn't it fun
To sit in the sun
But sometimes
My wish would be
To let my toes
Tingle
On the shingle.

My fingers grow blue
Change to another hue
My heart sings out
But inside my head
The bells jangle
And I have to say
Try as I might
It's no good tonight.

I'll just laugh at it all
And tomorrow
Will be
Alright.
Andrina Keeling

The Country Life
That's the life, the country life
Where some folks love to roam
To wander by the hills and streams
Many miles from home.

To hear the call of the curlew
Or catch sight of a wary stoat
Walk beside a quiet loch
And watch the swans afloat.

See the bleak and lonely moor
View a buzzard in the air
Watch sly old fox in search of food
To bring back to his lair.

Rabbits and hares are a common sight
And the magpie with its relations
With a bit of luck one can observe
Geese flying in formation.

That's the life, the country life
Where folks go at their leisure
Exploring nature's lovely things
What beautiful memories to treasure.
James Fleming

Lincolnshire

Lincolnshire, dear old Lincolnshire, the place of my home and birth.
There's no other county quite like it, the jewel of this fair earth.
The wolds with their sweeping hillsides, give beauty
                                         beyond compare.
The fens have a peace and tranquillity that no other county
                                         can share.

This precious word when spoken is sacred from the start,
To someone born in Lincolnshire, it grows within the heart.
Wherever life may lead you, wherever you must roam,
Your thoughts will always wander back to Lincolnshire, your home.

There are no rocky seashores, no mountains or no lakes,
But how that lush green countryside, much more than compensates.
And when God planned this garden, he made it very clear,
The Trent, the sea, the Humber, would keep its beauty here.

So when man built the bridges and made us Humberside,
He took away our heritage, he took away our pride.
Oh Lincolnshire we love you and will fight on to restore,
The boundaries of thee, dear county, to where they were before.
V M Goulding

A Birdseye View of East Anglia

The wind that blows across the Fens
Is fierce and strong and free.
Imagine you too are a bird
And glide across the fields with me.

In springtime, every year, I come
To find my clay daubed nest
Beneath the reed thatched brown beamed home
Of country folk I love the best.

The farmer tills the fine black soil,
His face brown tanned and lined,
Hopes no fen blow will take his crops,
And heavy rain clouds will be kind.

In summertime my brood I tend,
Skim o'er St Ives, see Cromwell's hand
Outstretched to point to market stalls,
Whilst farmers talk of beasts and land.

When autumn comes, the golden grain
Cascades from combines - plump rich wheat,
From Boston's Stump the view is grand,
A patchwork quilt of tates and beet.

An icy nip is in the air,
I know that winter soon will come,
Then snow will cover Norwich spires,
And drive the sheep flocks nearer home.

East Anglia! I love the sounds,
The sights of furrows straight and black,
And when I feel the call next spring
I'll gladly come. I will be back!
Dora K Tack

Ballschadden

In autumn days nay haunt no more
The echoes of a distant past
Where sea birds soar around your rugged crags
Where early mist thus shrouds your mournful face
And spring flowers greet the morning light.

Where poets great once trod this lonely place
In search of solance and of grace
Where men of vision ponder on your brow
The times gone by and those who dare to dream.

Where fern and heather scented slopes do sigh
And lovers pledge their through to him on high
Where kestrels sway on slip stream floating by
And muffins nest away from prying eye.

Ballschadden you're a barron place
Your sons desert you with such haste
The innocent their childish games do play
In youthful days they too have yet to say.
M McKenna

The Humber Bridge

Spanning the river in great majesty,
A glorious sight for all to see.
Was talked about for many a year,
A sight to behold, the bridge is here.

Made of concrete, and tons of steel,
It's got character, charm, and great appeal.
A world record holder of its kind,
A more splendid bridge hard to find.
British design, engineering and skill,
Worked together, a dream to fulfil.
Adorning the river with beauty and grace,
A benefit to workers and the holiday race.
Linking the north and south bank together,
The Humber bridge will stay forever.
Joyce Margaret Prescott

Night Sky

Alone, the shining evening star
Guides the way to night,
Waiting for her sisters' beams
To add their share of light
To heaven's darkened mantle
Soon starred to such a height
That man must stop, and
Wonder, at the sight.

Upon some other planet
Do watchers, such as we,
Likewise gaze and ponder
This starlit infinity?
'Tis known our learnéd ones insist
There is no life save we -
But, surely man is vain to think
The Gods made only he.
Sheila Grimwood

Homecoming

Whoever thought I'd live to see again
The little streets and black soil of the fen
The town that made and nurtured me
For many years was just a memory.

I've been so blessed - 'tis true to say
So many chances came my way
As over lands and seas I travelled
In God's fine world I looked and marvelled.

Now I am ageing - time is spent
My family was heaven sent
To help me to return back home
For no one soul should die alone.

To walk across the old canal
And wander 'round the modern mall
I gaze upon the roads that grew
A potpourri of old and new.

Still the bells of Peter chime
Across the town to warn the time
Is running out - so live, enjoy
And all your love and life employ.

It feels so good to be back home
I never wish again to roam
I am content - at peace to be
Where Norfolk voices call to me.
Sheila Goodman

War Widow

Tenderly,
So tenderly,
Weeping forty-year-old tears of love,
She traces out the name with bony fingers
In the cold, hard, granite stone.

Lovingly,
On bended knee,
She scatters scarlet flowers
On the new-mown grass
And rearranges them.

This holy spot,
So long unknown,
So infinitely long-imagined in her mind,
Becomes reality -
The here-and-now experience
Of her lonely self.

Beneath the scarlet flowers
Lies her aching heart;
She rises to her feet
And tearfully imparts a kiss
Upon the granite stone,
Still cold and hard.

The whispered messages,
Inaudible to all
Except her sleeping heart,
Re-echo far beyond the limitations
Of Eternity.
She turns away and walks
Across the grass
Towards reality.
G A James

A Plea From the Heart

A plea from the heart
Rings in souls of many
To release lasting peace
And to sustain harmony.

Tears through terrorism
Fills wells of humanity,
The British people seek only
to join hands and find unity.

Bombs must not explode
And children must not die,
The words must be found
For love ones not to cry.

Now we may be along way
But a beginning lies ahead,
Let's talk and find an answer
In remembrance for the dead.

Now politics of the world
Have descended upon our land,
It's time to stop all conflicts
And to unite and make a stand.
Derek Dean

Cry of the Hungry Child

In a world that has sent men to the moon
Why should I sit here with an empty spoon?
I'm hungry, I'm starving, I'm craving for some food
My mum has sold my clothes and I am nude.

How long will I live, when will I die?
How long before I join my sisters in the sky?
I'm hungry, I've got no food to eat
I'm hungry, I've got no shoes on my feet
I'm hungry,
I'm hungry for some food

In a world that gets smaller every day
Where the workers are always after more pay
Where Concorde can fly at twice the speed of sound
I sit here starving on the ground

How long will I live?
When will I die?
How long before I join my sisters in the sky?
Rodney George Priest

Greenpeace

Who are we to scream and shout of our quality of life,
Just look about.
Many creatures large and small, have no homes,
No food at all.
The animal kingdom becomes fragile and rare because we
Uproot trees and leave the ground bare.

Take the koala and the panda bear too, one has no shelter
The other, no bamboo.
The fabulous eagle, no more on the wing, it's us
We've done this terrible thing.
We take their eggs, their chicks don't thrive
How on earth can they stay alive.

Return to earth all we take, we must put right
This big mistake.
The elephants and tigers, they need their space
Why should their existence become a race?
The deer and the bison have a right to roam, the monkeys
And baboons they deserve a home.

Listen to the animals, then moan and shout, the quality of their
Lives, that's what it's about.
Don't let it get any worse, we are all here to share
The same universe
Think again about what we do, it's up to me and it's up to you
Take good care of this God given ground
Or in the future (there will be) no animals to be found.
Jenni Brown

Gulf War

A bird, it was
it cried because
The sun had gone.

It tried to swim
would not give in
it couldn't win.
The sun had gone.

It tried to fly
to stay alive
could not survive,
Because the sun had gone.

No! No nuclear bomb,
just oil pollution.
That's why the sun had gone.

Then human hands came urgent
with tons of detergent.
Hands repaired and then prepared
For the bird to glide fly run
To find the sun.
Diane Hasler

Truth

Make believe in games we play
Of soldiers and of dolls
In stories that are told to us
The magic that unfolds,
We live our lives in daydreams
With music to our ears
We plant the seeds of happiness
For all the coming years.
Though try as might we cannot see
Deep sorrow in their eyes
Of broken dreams and shattered lives
Of pastures that have been
The wars and battles plenty
Our seeking to bear fruit
Little does the child that knows
A stranger at his feet.
Valerie A Preston

11th November

I saw the hills were full of poppies
The fields below were covered too.
The bright red poppies seem to be dancing
up and down the poppy hill.
Can I hear? Do I imagine all those voices
from beneath the hills.
It's all those brave men, they are singing
Bob, Tom, Jack and Bill.
Down beneath all those poppies are the
Graves of these brave men.
Brothers, lovers, sons and fathers all
buried down below.
Is this not a warning, to us people
up above.

Please don't take a life that God has given
Just fill your hearts with peace, and love
Then perhaps the fields of flanders
and the poppies on the hills.
And all those brothers, sons and lovers
and all those fathers too.
Will then know, that their lives
Weren't spent for nothing.
Remember that they gave their lives
for you.
Rita Dicks

Ireland

Oh Ireland this troubled land
There will be no peace with gun in hand.
Oh let the children go out in the streets to play
Fill their hearts with love, and let them stay
Oh put away your guns and bombs.
Let all religions have peace and joy
Sing your nice songs like *Danny Boy.*
Oh put your guns away
Put out your hands to your neighbour all around
This is how peace is found.
Oh put your guns away.

D Iggulden

No More Wars

No more discrimination
No more explanation
No more war of words
No more religious vows.

No more degradation
No more salutation
No more bullets
No more wars.

We thought the war was over
Now we can see green shamrock
Mortars and bobby traps
Aimed to kill.

The police are up in arms
Divided against religion's harm
We thought the war was over
Now the soldiers roll in clover.

No more wars
No more salutation
No more bullets
We thought the war was over.
Alison Rumgay

An Inspiring Rain
(For Nicola)

On a starry crystal night
With the radiant moon
beaming to be my lonesome light,
Colonies of young and old
large or small tears of rain
Splash then softly beat romantically untold
against my heart's thrashing pain.

Each running course of a drop
Wriggles in a vigorous race
like Vincent's expressive brush top
With its emotionally tortured pace.

My horizon line is now a chrysalis of slippery lizard's skin
Which is highlighted by the fluorescent moles that dwell within.
A reptilian crucifix is held
by my evolving window frame
and the euphoric pleasures it yelled
were not merely a game.

From looking to the sky bright lights stain my eyes,
they leave their impression and then withdraw my lies
And as each new wet drop claims a dry
the light of a raindrop is the sight of a fly.

Hazy street lamps outline my view as would a globe
the outer wounded window with my touch I probe
I outstretch my arm towards the colour spectrum
A raindrop baby hangs lazily from my thumb
the drip looks at me and winks
its body consistency being an infinite palette of eyes, peering,
anxious for sight.
As the rain bruises the glass on this wet, dismal night.
Luke Palmer

Spring

Awake! Cold earth,
Do not be fooled when cold wind blow
Awake! 'Tis spring.

Cannot you feel the sun's warm rays?
Cheering your very heart.
Awake! Take off thy shroud
And play your gallant part.

Each little bird on hedge and tree
All bursting out so vigorously
The spring rains, each drop of dew
Will make a lovely sight of you.

The snowdrops and primroses
Are blooming in my garden
A welcome sight, there is no doubt,
When mother nature first steps out.

Each little flower that grows
Each little bird that sings
Each have a meaning of their own
And welcome in the spring.

Soon the cuckoo will be heard
As he flies from tree to tree
We long to hear his joyful note
I know you must agree.

Yes, awake, cold earth from your winter sleep,
Roll out your carpet of green
The sun shines bright and the wind blows warm,
You've God's miracle to perform.
O C Dunn

It's Spring Again
When December snow flakes fall
What do they bring us one and all
in a few months time after snow and rain
it will be spring once more again.

When the snow has gone
and flowers appear
as the seasons change
it's another year.

What a miserable place
this world would be
if there were no flowers
each day to see.

So when December returns again
With icy snow and pouring rain
Just around the corner is an open door
and we find spring is here again once more.
E Warren

Autumn Leaves

Look how they flutter to the ground
The leaves of orange, bronze and brown
There they rustle at our feet
Their mission now is complete,
All their glory dead and gone
The November winds blow them along
There they drift into little heaps
Trod on in the busy streets.
Bare trees lift their heads to the sky
As if in pity they do cry
Where! As all our splendour gone
There's nothing left for us but the birds' song.
Norah Reeves

Bread and Childhood

Me and my gas mask tin started infants school
on the same day in 1940.
Come to think of it, we were never far away
from each other for the next five years.
Our mam said times were hard, what with
the food rationing and all that.
We often had bread and lard for tea, but
to be honest, I acquired quite a taste for it.
Well, you couldn't waste anything in those days.
Mam said it was like feeding the devil if
you threw away any bread,
what with so many people dead or dying
so we could all be free.
Sometimes, though, at Sunday tea we had
tinned fruit, but mam made us all eat bread
with that, yet nobody seemed to get fat, so
I suppose it must have *done us good*.
Remember eating chewing-wood in the streets
because there weren't any sweets to buy?

When I hear today's toddlers cry for them in
supermarkets, it makes me wild and
I want to say, 'You should have been a child
in *my* day!'
Mind you, we never seemed unhappy
and I often wonder why our mam said
times were very bad.
I just remember all that bread
and loving mam and dad.
Shirley Frances Winskill

Unsettled Mind

It's not the snow that makes you cold,
It's more the fear of growing old,
In a greedy world which has grown so fast,
And its very existence, doubts are cast.
Before the days of vicious wars,
You could live in peace, with no locked doors.
So if ever I could live again,
Maybe it would be sometime when,
You could walk in fields of grass and roses,
And sail the river, just like Moses.
Live in a house made out of bramble,
Up and down the hills I'd scramble,
To hunt for food, and rest your head,
Wherever you wished, but let it be said,
There'd be no birth control, or extended play,
And no Beatles, singing *'She loves you yeh, yeh, yeh,'*
No squash to play, or learning to ski,
No Honda, Suzuki or Kawasaki,
If only, if only, what could I do?
I want the past, the future too.
If only I had a settled mind.

Perhaps one day in my life I'll find,
The utopia for which I'm searching,
Instead of my mind endlessly perching,
On the precipice of going insane,
Maybe then it would be the snow that makes you cold,
Instead of the fear of growing old.
Terry Watson

Memories

We can never go back to the place we once knew
Or try to recapture our youth.
The people are changed, the buildings are gone,
Now skyscrapers spoil the view.
Just think of the towns and the countries so neat,
Nestled amongst hill and dell.
All we get now are lorries and cars,
It's almost like living in hell.
Our hearts are so full of our sweet memories,
Our nostalgic thoughts must cease.
From our life as it was, to what it is now,
It is time for our souls to find peace.
We must give up our thoughts of days gone by,
So don't be morose and sad.
Just hold our heads high, and laugh at the world,
Be peaceful, happy and glad
We don't have to think of this land of ours,
It belongs to this planet called earth.
So we just settle down, be glad we're alive,
As this planet's the land of our birth.
Lily M Shipley

Life's Stock Market

We enter life with nothing, but a dividend of days,
Like stocks and shares they fluctuate in many different ways,
We reach our teens, and gaily toss each day across our shoulder,
We're thirty, and we're pulled up sharp, we feel we're getting older,
Then suddenly, we're forty, where did the good years go?
Before we turn, we're fifty, and the grey begins to show.
We're sixty, and grandparents now, the *market's* on the down trend,
At seventy we realise that every day's a godsend.
Turned eighty, we begin to think that on us lies the onus,
Of making what we can of life, for every day's a bonus,
For when at last we reach the *Gate*, despite all corner cutting,
We're passing through with what we brought, approximately *nothing*.
C Chapman

Child's Play

Mothers parted from their sons
Babies born to the sound of guns.
Children far and wide and near
Beg protection from their fear.

Pillage, rape, in war torn lands
Wicked deeds by evil hands.
Racial hatred, widespread, rife
With scant respect for human life.

Vengeful men, old scores to settle
Rain down on children shards of metal
Robbing them of limbs, and eyes
Oblivious to their anguished cries.

When will this inhumanity cease
When will our planet know true peace?
Things are bad and times are rough
Let's call a halt. Enough's enough.

42

The solution is within our grasp
Put others first, and self last.
Heed the commandment. Love all others
Goodwill show to sisters, brothers.

Universal caring must be applied
To save this earth from genocide.
Our broken world could be renewed
With no more heartache, pain and feud.

No more suffering, no more tears,
Guns silenced, banished fears.
Shrieks of laughter to fill the day
With rapturous unabashed, child's play.
Barbara Eastham

Every Day Blues
We cannot face up to turn on the TV,
for we're so scared of what we may see.
It breaks our hearts when we see the news,
for there's nothing good, just every day blues.
People just don't seem to care any more,
I get frightened by the thought,
violent, abusive people, there's so many of this sort.
What will come to this world I'm ashamed to live in,
to change it, to make it better,
just where would we begin!
Lisa Marie Stott

Juggling Politicians
The good news today
So the authorities say,
Unemployment is falling -
If that is so - I would like to know
Can they be stalling?

43

The bad news is - we all agree
Prisons are full to capacity
Overcrowded, as never before
Bursting at the seams
Can't hold any more.

It occurs to me and I surmise
When the prisoners are free
On the dole queue they'll be
So, it's no surprise, unemployment will rise.
Then the mathematical magicians
And clever politicians
Will conjure up figures galore
And juggle statistics once more.
Peggy Moore

Bosnia

If this is dawn, whose fingers feel my face,
I wish to die, my heart for to embrace
A greater love than this. My baby sucks
My breast, huddled amidst the sounds of strife
Which shatter remnants of another life.
We doze, and then awake, un-nerved,
As silence creeps upon the town, unheard,
And people move regardless of their race,
Their creed, they are neighbours in urgent mood
United in their need, our need for food.
A shell explodes as daylight splinters through
I think of family, country I once knew
Now scarred, and I with all my strength ask why?
The blinds are drawn on those who died in mud
And even now life ebbs, while child sucks blood.
Felicity Robinson

Human Emotions

Human emotions run deep in this world of ours
Violence, crime everything imaginable in twenty four hours.
Years come fast and go
We never learn that man is the lowest of the low.
Greed is the only thing he knows,
Wiping human life off the face of the earth in countless blows.
What has man learned from living and life,
He just might as well stabb the world with a knife.
If the world was a balloon
It would pop and shatter into a trillion moons
Then maybe it would bring about a form of peace,
and a new human race
for kind loving emotion to release.
Dawn M Kingsbury

A Northern Ireland Dream

The children were happy today
No more bombs! Or explosions
Families were having good times
The sun was always shining
And the sky was always blue
Never *black* the way we knew.
Everyone was smiling, never crying
The pain had gone away
Those men with their guns had gone
And the curfews had stopped
People could start living again
Their freedom had returned
Then I awoke and I heard a loud noise
It was just a Northern Ireland dream
Maybe it will come true for you and me
          I hope so!
Victoria Sutton (15)

Hiroshima

Glaring out of my window
Looking all around
Yet I'm seeing nothing
Though there's plenty around
I'm dreaming of a faraway land
Hiroshima to be exact
Hiroshima the place of that terrible attack.
It was the atom bomb we know
We knew before it dropped
An American bomber named *Enola Gay*
Enola Gay, is that a fact,
It was early one morning in August
We know it had to be done
It saved the life of millions
Those Japs under *The sun*
I went myself to see it
A few years after it dropped
And by God I can tell you
It certainly made me stop!
I shall never forget it
Not as long as I live
I wish I had never gone there
I wish I had never lived,
Because since I left there
I've been in a perpetual dream
Remembering a little boy *melted*
Just like a soft ice cream.
Will they ever forgive us?
I can't see how they can
Can they ever forgive us
Those people from Japan
W Howes

46

A Tory Tale

I must admit
You've done your bit
My bank balance is healthy,
My luxury home
Is all my own
Tho' I wouldn't call me wealthy
Our L reg: Mercs'
(The hidden perks)
We only use for pleasure
My chauffeur driven
Daimler is
For business not for leisure.
I'm pleased to say
My *take home pay*
Has recently improved
With John's consent,
By 70%.
So poverty is removed
All thanks to you
My loyal crew
My future is assured
But sad to say
You've had your day
A fact to be deplored.
You have your skills
Intangibles?
A pity they are wasted,
No doubt this news
Will blow a fuse
And leave you devastated.

Redundancy
You'll take today
I'm sorry by you'll *have ter*
Make this your goal
Collect your dole
Live happy ever after.

Dot T Robinson

A Far Walk From Bosnia

As I walk step by step in the icy snow
I wrap my coat around me wondering which way to go.
The snow is falling on my face, my hands are freezing too,
This is the month of Christmas time, I just don't know what to do
But I wish you merry Christmas and a happy new year to you.

As I walk step by step in the icy snow,
I can hear some children singing - and laughing as they go.
Their singing Christmas carols, good will to all mankind
I only want a little help, but that I cannot find.

As I walk step by step in the lonely street
The snow keeps on falling and twirling around my feet.
I just keep on walking to see what I might find
If it's just someone to talk to, to be gentle, to be kind.

As I walk step by step in the icy snow
I look up to the sky and the stars are aglow.
The moon is still shining but the clouds are closing in
It won't be long before night falls, it'll be so dark and grim.
I'm feeling rather tired now and my feet are freezing cold
But I will keep on walking till I find a path of gold.
I just don't know what to do
But I wish you a merry Christmas and a happy new year to you.

As I walk step by step in the icy snow,
I wish someone would take my hand to show me which way to go
The night time is almost here, as my eyes close I shed a tear
But then I feel great warmth around me and my heart is aglow.
I know now where I'm going, no more walking in the snow
I'm going up to heaven, where all the poor kids go.
Now I am an angel, I'm with Jesus that is true,
But I wish you merry Christmas and a happy new year to you.
Christine Makin

All Over Again

The war is over,
The fighting's done
The war is over,
Both lost, and won.
The dust has settled
On the battle ground,
Now all silent,
No more sound.

War has no winners
War has no losers
We all win,
We all lose
In that way,
Between both sides,
Nothing, to choose.

All bury our dead,
Come the dawn
Both loser, and victor
Our lost comrades, we mourn,
Now we must live
With our memories
Live with, our sorrow, and pain
Rebuild our lives, and countries
Until it starts,
All over again.
James Molineaux Starr

Six Days in June - 1967

He'd left his wife and little ones,
The call had been so strong;
The war would only be short they had said,
He was sure that he wouldn't be long.

Oh! He was right that soldier,
That soldier so young and brave,
For him the war was very short
Too soon he lay in his grave.

His wife and little ones were left alone
No daddy to sing them a song
All because the war was short
And he knew he wouldn't be long.
Sylvia Lukeman

A Small Part in it all
Muddy seawater, more akin to sewage,
born by mistakes,
All its life and essence,
now mingled with death.
In a farm of noxious flow,
the goldfish in plastic bags, will never know,
Even if they live to see,
the desperation of the tourists,
Putting back on their clothes in disgust,
wondering where is left to go.
Is *everything* blind?
Donkeys chained,
Don't walk on the grass,
every seedling carefully sown,
Nature is unemployed,
Soon she'll be a memory,
there's too many people in this place,
Too much to throw away
it's just the price we have to pay,
For having a small part, in it all
the money man with his cigarettes, his
potted plants, his secret police,
Supports the cause, that causes the wars
now there's too many to kill,

Hence, bigger bombs,
nature's tried and tried,
But man's work is on a different path.
At last the donkey will become untied,
the goldfish it will swim outside,
as freedom becomes incidental,
to a greater illness.
Yvvette M Ogden

Bosnia

Insanity breathes its foul pestilence across the once fruitful terrain.
The scorched horizons, barren through plagues of madness
lie lifeless, tired and spent.
There is no shelter from the unforgiving elements, and the stale earth
offers no sound of water.
The minds of millions drape from the fractured boughs of the
sap-starved trees that once nourished them.
The pain and the anguish blow across the stony wasteland where the
mere essence of life runs scarce.
The hopes of a world hang on the wind.
Shadows flock to the crude, pathetic markers we few remember
as friends.
They were the fortunate ones.
Even the scavengers and parasites who once drank our mealy
corpses dry have since gone.
There is little time left.
Our disease conquers all.
Am I part of this vapid landscape or a diabolical extension of a
freakish mind rendered derelict by the brutality of its society.
Maybe this land is a creation of my own subconscious, a fantastic
nightmare fuelled by the negativity of thought.
I breathe, but is it air that I inhale or is it the vaporous toxin spewed
by Satan himself.
Has my time come, is my pact with darkness complete.

I sense the arrival, I smell the putrid stench of Death himself,
and taste his pungent excreta on my lips.
Am I already his servant, and he my master.
Maybe I am dead. I must be.
I live in Hell.
Robin Lawson

Liberty

It wasn't easy in the desert heat,
With scuds a falling down in the street.
People would run when the sirens would blare,
Our allied pilots sorties they'd dare,
They'd fly to the night not sure of their fate,
It was just their job to capture Kuwait,
For the lads on the land, they'd keep in their ranks,
Saricens, jeeps and challenger tanks.
British or American, their aim was the same,
To topple that tyrant *Saddam Hussein*.
Shaun McDowell

Northern Ireland - Echoes of a Troubled Land

Bang, bang are the echoes of the night!
Bang, bang and not even a fight,
Blood, tears, death and despair
and once again we are all filled with fear!

Churches full with people mourn
and more sad memories there are born,
Flowers are placed to represent respect
Coffins are placed to hide the dead,
what follows but words left unsaid!

God waits at heaven's door
where we go for peace - not war!
Regardless of our age, sex, race or *religion*,
Not one of us is allowed to sin
once we meet up with the almighty kin.

But what about the sinful ones
left living in our world?
Innocent beings tasting the bitter pill
of religion!

The dead have lost
but who has won?
No-one but a deadly *bomb!*

And what must we tell
our tomorrow's child?
The *truth* -
That the *world* has gone *wild!*
Jayne Marie Mottram

Lament From the Future
They grew they said
From the earth they said
Tall and green to the sky they said,
Trees they called them
The old ones saw them
And watched them die.

But we have things that
rise from the ground
Spires and cones, squares
and rounds
In beautiful colours so why
should we cry
Ah! But to grow from the ground.

53

To bud and to leaf
To turn to gold then shed
its load
To know for sure when
spring returns
It will grow again
Oh this cold earth from
which life came
Will it ever see a tree again?
Betty Hand

Why

Why are we always at war?
What the hell is it for?

Soldiers come and strip the
           land
burying mines deep in the sand.

Killing each other the human race
they'll press the button and be no trace,

There's rape and murder every day
surely life's not meant to be that way.

What's wrong with living in peace
when's all the corruption going to cease.

Whatever our colour it's all the same
everybody's in on the sordid game.

Why can't we love and all be friends
who's going to dream up the next sick trend.

The world could be a lot better place
let's work together in making it safe.

Why are we always at war?
somebody tell me what we're doing
             it for.
Lorraine Heath

Spiritual Wanderings
The storm flashed its fury across the sky
Throwing lightning down from its angry eye
The swamps darkened under the swirling mist
While thunder thrashed its violent fist.

The house stood alone on top of the hill
Wind raged around it, deafening and shrill
Trees rattled their branches on window panes
While death crept stealthily around the rain.

With icy fingers death traced the man's face
With intimate knowledge it found the place
To release the man's spirit into the air
Where hovering above, it gazed on those there.

Oh wicked fate! Why him, they cry
Haven't you enough of people who die?
Their sobs of bereavement drown in the storm
While, unseen by them, others take form.

Come now my son, it's time to go
Your mother is waiting with others you know
A new life is written, a different day
Follow closely, we'll show you the way.

Hell rages beneath giving vent to its wrath
Vile curses stream from its evil mouth
His anger at losing yet another soul
His collection of bodies a consummate goal.

Higher and higher the spirits flee the night
Travelling till reaching the bursting of light
Where night opens up and sweet music plays
Where virtue finds peace at the end of life's day.
Sandra Glendenning

Flowers

Flowers are beautiful,
Flowers are sweet,
Flowers are colourful,
Making a gardener's dream complete!
Susan A Watson (10)

Dawn Chorus

Softly starts at end of night
In the dawning's early light
Birds awaken in the spring
Early mornings listening.

Have you heard their chorus sweet
As another day they greet
Even in the town you hear
Songs of love so sweet and clear.

Sharing with us all around
In the joyful swelling sound
Makes us glad to be alive
As we hear the day arrive.

What a blessing we can say
For another lovely day
With the birthing of the morn'
In the chorus of the dawn.
Leonora Steele

Farewell to Daylight

Surveying the rolling landscape
As I sit up on the Downs,
I can see the ocean in the distance
Villages, wood and towns.
The church spires pointing towards the sky
Cattle grazing in the fields,
Farmers working on the land
Harvesting the summer yields.
Streams that shimmer in the sun
A train travelling at high speed,
In the sky birds are gracefully flying
Searching for things on which to feed.
Way out on the horizon
This ships seem to disappear,
As they sail towards their destination
Evening starts to draw near.
When dusk begins to gather round me
The towns and villages are aglow,
And there's something about just sitting there watching
As the daylight starts to go.
A calmness descends with arrival of night
And a blanket of stars cover the sky,
Then the moon lights my way
As I journey home
Whispering a silent goodbye.
Pat Frampton

All Kinds of Flowers

Beautiful flowers, I love them all
Sweet-scented wallflowers shaded by the wall,
Daisies so white and each petal fresh
The fine lacy flowers of baby's breath,
Pansies with painted faces aglow
Sit next to the alyssum all in a row,
Marigolds of orange hue so bright
Tobacco plants that smell lovely at night.

57

Aromatic lavender of deep purplish blue
Bluebells I see in the woods I walk through,
Vinginian stocks with confetti like flowers
Little forget-me-nots nestling in bowers,
Jasmine and daffodils, radiant in yellow
Delicate freesia, a very good seller,
Tulips, known several centuries ago
Standing like soldiers all in a row.

Hollyhocks, delphinium, sunflowers tall
Snowdrops, crocus, and violets so small,
Honeysuckle, clematis, how they entwine,
Twisting and turning like columbine,
The king of all flowers the rose to be sure
Such divine blooms in colours galore,
Proud dahlia's a hybrid so pure
A bouquet of flowers is like a good cure.

Hundreds and hundreds of volumes of flowers
To go through them all, would take many hours
But my favourite of all, yet modest to some
Is the pretty primrose, my top number one.
J Gowan

Winter Light
The silver blue river,
Sun shining so bright.
Then the cold winter air,
Strikes in the night.
The moon comes out
And the stars give their light,
But again in the morning,
The sun shines so bright.
Helene M Verrall (9)

58

Bright Star

At morningtide when air is fresh
And sparkling like the grass,
Then up above me, hanging there-
A diamond in blue glass.

The Evening Star in majesty
Awaits the coming dawn,
And as she does the pink-flushed clouds
Announce the day is born.

The sun, to take his place in might
Has now arrived, it seems
And Bright Star gathers up her light
And sails to secret dreams.

The day wears on full hot and steamy
Autumn nearly here.
Quietly the heat subsides
And chilly winds are near.

The sun is moving over now
Full gold and misty clothed,
All is still - so very still
It seemed that nothing moved.

The earth stood breathless
Round the bed of this the dying day,
Until at last with silent breath
It quietly slipped away.

The chilly evening made me pull
The curtains o'er the pane,
When looking up, I did espy
The Bright Star - back again!
Joan Deaves

Rain

The sky turns to grey and black,
The rain splashes on my back,
The rain is damp, the rain is fresh,
The water patters on my flesh.

The rain is sparkling, the rain is damp,
The cold wet drops shine like a lamp.
The water splashes,
The lightning flashes.

Pitter patter, splitter splatter,
I'm all wet! It doesn't matter.
Sparkle trickle splish! Splosh!
I want to put on my mackintosh.

The squashed up purple cloud,
The sound of the rain is very loud.
I hear splashing, I hear thunder,
I love the rain that I am under.
Debbie Hayes (8)

Autumn

A carpet laid of gold and browns
a fiery sunset on amber downs,
the trees stand solemn stark and bare
as the season changes without care.
I feel sorrow, my heart is sad
for I remember when the trees were clad
in leaves, all of the brightest green,
the summer walks where willows lean
their arched boughs, with poised finger tips
gently touching the stream, as it slips
thro' the meadows and far away
to where the nymphs and sylvans play.

A gentle rain falls from the skies
like the gentle tears that fill my eyes
for winter's nigh, to bring the snows
and the icy wind that endless blows,
a cape of white to cover the downs
that sparkle like jewels in majestic crowns.
S J Davies

Our Hedgehog

Selecting that place looking to my future
In the shed, in the greenhouse,
or in which your bonfire will make
A safe and sheltered spot I'll take.
Life becomes busy now, being continually alert
Pacing the days with time to assert
Finding old bits of plastic and dead leaves to combine
Which will make home in winter - just fine
Rolled up cosy like a scotch egg or two
You know, it's not any old thing which will do.

Thanks for my titbits and welfare concern
From my family and friend, he's called, *Ern*
You've thought of everything, we've really eaten well
So thanks for your friendship - I mean it sincerely
Nice people you are, I know I can tell.
Time is precious - we love you so dearly.
Let's hope winter's not too hard
I know you'll want to be my guard
Anyway, I'll make my bed really nice and tight
With luck I should be alright.

When next spring comes so fresh and green
I'll come to see you - you'll know where I've been
But before I sleep these months ahead
I must say, 'It's a pleasure to do business with you,'
I hope you'll know I'm not dead.

Oh! Bye the way, next year, please
If we see you out and about, without trees
Particularly when you're in your car
Can you avoid us? So we can go far,
Our little legs won't carry us, at speed, Tat - ah.
Leonard G Wordley

Summer

Those childhood days of summer when the earth
seemed to pant.
The grass was scorched and golden, the soil
alive with ants.
They used to march like soldiers in their
search for aphis fly.
Those never tiring Trojans as we watched
them trooping by.

The roe deer sought cool cover from the
midday sun's strong beat.
Ancient oaks their solace from the
penetrating heat.
We used to ramble freely in nature's
wonderland.
Always finding knowledge of things we
hadn't planned.

Water lilies on the lake caressed by
dragon flies blue.
The transparency of their gossamer wings
brought out another hue.
The small brick bridge close by the
stream where we splashed in waters cool.
The moor hens with their baby chicks on
Croxten's Mill pool.

The magic of the grass snake as he shed
his last year's skin.
We wished that we could do the same and
feel as cool as him.
Those childhood days of summer when
everything seemed new.
Now often seem an age away, but then
a dream come true.
Valerie Deacon

The Fox

While walking in the woods today,
I spied a fox along the way.
With coat of red and eyes of gold
A lovely lady to behold.
She held her bushy tail on high,
A silhouette against the sky.
She turned to look into my face,
A creature proud and full of grace.
That glance I know was more a plea,
It said you must not follow me.
For in the distance I could hear,
Her hungry cubs, their calls were clear.
I headed home, and never will
Tell of that glance on Danbury Hill.
Evelyn Gladstone

Primrose

I am a wayside flower
Nestling in the grass
No one seems to notice me
As they hurry past.

I am a pretty primrose
Adorning the path
Why don't people notice me
As they hurry past.

63

Yellow head shining brightly
Up towards the sky
No one seems to notice me
As they hurry past.

Why is everyone so busy
To spend the time of day
Looking at a wayside flower
Nestling in the grass.

My yellow head is drooping
My days are nearly passed
Why haven't people noticed me
As they hurried past.

To see the beauty that there is
Is all I ask of you
Just keep your eyes wide open
As you hurry past.

Eunice Cherry

My Feathered Friends

In spring my feathered friends wake at dawn,
I feed them early in the morn,
Cheeky sparrows peck at my door,
Like Oliver, they must be asking for more.

In my trees baby birds *cheep, cheep,*
Mother blackbird gives them something to eat,
Noisy starlings fly around,
Picking any scraps on the ground.

Little robin redbreast stately and serene,
Is the prettiest little bird ever seen,
Hopping along with his bright red breast,
Looking for crumbs the others have left.

My feathered friends in winter,
Are so hungry and poor,
I feed them every morning,
Outside my kitchen door.

I peep through the window,
What a pretty sight,
To see them feeding, flapping wings,
Some even having a fight.

They fly away contented and chirping,
I know just what they say,
'Thank-you,
See you again, another day.'

I watch with interest this friendly trend,
How proud I am to be their friend.
Margery English

The Storm
Peals of thunder, coruscating lightning,
rend the night sky asunder.
Ascending through the riven air,
the song of church bells, tolls amidst
the threnody of chaos.

Corpuscular fires chase the scudding clouds,
torn to ribbons by razors of cold
moonlight from above.

The obeisant canopies of trees,
laden by torrents of lachrymose waters,
hang towards the recently parched ground,
her scars and wounds, inflicted by solar fury;
now instantly healed and obliterated by the gushing
rivulets of a baptismal anointing
she had been so long denied.

The ether of healing earth is
a rich and heady pungency
which fills the senses with
an awareness of resurgent vitalities.

This picture of violent night is
riven in two by a spear of lightning,
a shaft of silver wrath from the low and
ominous clouds.

Within the warrens of small creatures
and in the shelters of men,
a startled state of semi-consciousness presides,
as all, apprehensively await
the earth to re-balance her
disparate energies:
Mark Rogers

Our Garden

The squirrel's on the garden fence
   the doves are in the tree.

While starlings flying here and there
   are searching for their tea.

The blackbird and the greenfinch
   are looking 'round for bits.

Seen peeping from the laurel
   the robins and blue tits.

The thrushes and the magpie
   sometimes a pink jay.

All frequent our garden
   to brighten up each day.
Muriel Richards

66

The Wonder of Spring

A distant cuckoo calls and wakes the thrush,
A blackbird starts to sing then with a rush
The air is full of music loud and clear,
And suddenly I know that spring is here.

Sun shining through the trees, grass wet with dew,
The air is fresh and clean and everything looks new,
My heart's so full of joy I want to sing,
For winter's gone, and suddenly it's spring.

Lambs gambol in the fields, and down the lane
Buttercups and daisies bloom again.
Birds, butterflies and bees are on the wing,
Lord, thank you for the miracle of spring.
Olive Peever

Harvest Time

It's wonderful to see
the fields of golden grain
Soon the fields will be quite bare
When the harvesting is done
A crisp cool nip is in the air
As we stroll along the lane
Mist has spread across the fields
It almost looks like rain
We hope it soon will go away
Till they've gathered in the grain.

It's sad to see the summer days
Get shorter every day
Then the nights darker
Bringing winter on its way,
With snow to cover all the fields
And keep the ground so warm

Till spring comes around again
And seeds are sown once more
Soon the summer days will come
We will stroll along the lanes
To see again that lovely sight
The fields of golden grain.
I Boyden

Autumn

When the days begin to shorten
And some birds fly far away,
Then autumn is arriving
Its special beauty to display.

Soon the trees will be dressed
In russet red and gold,
And we will go for country walks
Their beauty to behold.

The harvest will be gathered in
Ripe fruits and golden corn.
Then leaves will fall to carpet the earth
And mist will shroud the dawn.

The squirrel will hasten to hide his store
The hedgehog will bury deep.
Nature is preparing
For its winter sleep.

Autumn is a special time
Created for your pleasure,
Notice the changes that it brings
They are for you - to treasure.
Hazel Taylor

Autumn Glory

How beautiful are the mellow autumn days,
Filling our earth, with joy, and songs of praise,
For all the wonders, of God's world around.
Where beauty, and colour, in profusion abound.

Red, yellow and gold, and every pretty tint,
Such wondrous glory, should make our hearts think,
The shining beauty of each sunset fair,
God's power, and might, are revealed *Just there*.

All around us, are the *wonders of his love*
Every precious gift *is from our God above*
Spring, autumn, winter, with all their beauty show,
What *he has given to us,* here on earth below.

And the autumn of life, as it comes to all,
As the leaves of life, *gently to earth fall*
We have *a glory* which keeps bright within.
An eternal life, where heaven's joys begin,

Though our outward man perish as the falling leaves,
We shall gather, and bring in the sheaves,
Through *God's salvation* given through his dear son
Eternity within us, *the true life has begun.*

Life which never fades, and never will pass away
Becomes ours, and everlasting day
The life within us, is renewed *all the time*
Love, and peace, and joy, and graciousness divine

Understanding, tolerance, and *God's wondrous love*
Patience, perseverance, *his gifts from heaven above,*
Our lives become mellowed, *made, like unto him*
An eternal glory, which will never, never dim.

Made into *his likeness* as we love him day by day,
Guided, and kept, along life's unknown way,
His love transforms, our every action here,
Until *complete, in his image, our lives shall appear.*
Doris L Middleditch

Summer Season

Golden yellow sun to blind us,
With its permeating rays;
Misty mornings, slow unveiling,
Golden-downsoft - summer days.
Drifting fields of sunripe wheat ears,
Pleasuring the eyes to see,
Gardens full of summer flowers,
Fruit, and butterflies and bees,
Blossom trees, their colours blaze,
Lift laden limbs up to the sky,
As if to thank their Lord the sun,
Until the summer passes by.
Maureen Rule

An Actor's Life for Me!

We're on the stage and dancing,
We're on bowing or romancing,
A life of arts we're chancing,
To make the break someday.
A film, a dance, or play.
To take ourselves away,
And reach fortune and fame,
Ourselves a household name,
And acting is the game.

The camera keeps on turning,
Your lines you are slowly learning,
The midnight oil is burning,
As you slowly fade to sleep.
Your dreams they run so deep,
In your actor's life you keep.
And you wake up in the sun,
Suspended dreams, they're hung
In galleries of fun.

The curtain slowly rises,
The actors in disguises,
A stage full of surprises,
And as the curtain falls,
The people in the stalls,
In ovation, standing tall.
And you take the final bow,
Overcome right now,
You made it through somehow!
Brian J Singer

What if I
What if I
stalked old ground still new
thought of now times past.
What if I
took a deliberate chance
came back though I never went.
What if I
tried hard for no effort
gave all to a no taker.
What if I
Hoped you weren't without love.
What if I
Lost someone already found?
S J Flynn

Look Around

If to you time goes slowly by,
just ask yourself the reason why,
Is it because your interest you have lost?
In things around you, then don't count the cost,
just look around, and pleasure find,
abound around you in every kind,
the birds that sing, the sun that shines,
herald a new day, as you draw the blinds.

Then it all depends on you,
start the day, and see it through,
in a new way, yep! wear a smile,
take an interest in others,
and talk awhile,
then the time will slip away,
not just once, but every day.
Leslie F Dukes

Feelings

I must change my life before it's too late,
You know there are days I really do hate,
Lonely and unhappy I am inside,
Feeling I am trying to hide.
I've got to get out of this rut I'm in,
I know it's something I've got to win,
To live life again and live life to the full,
Instead of feeling drab and dull.

Feelings of loneliness I feel inside,
Feelings of wanting to be loved I cannot hide,
The lonely days I spend alone,
Inside this empty house I call my home.
C A Waldron

Love at First Sight
The path climbed steep from Swale Bridge
My first lone walk, over Applegarth Ridge,
The bustle of town soon slipped away
And my only friends, spring lambs at play.

After three long miles, the glistening scar
Beckoned me onwards, but oh, so far
And below me now the winding Swale
A silver ribbon, through distant dale.

The yellow waymarks, on trees and stiles
Gave precious comfort for miles and miles
A deafening silence filled the air
Alone on the fell, a sudden fear.

Eyes fixed ahead, seeking the inn
Then a worried frown became a grin
The whitewashed walls, the simple light,
Yes it really was, love at first sight.
Brian Lawmon

Memories
I remember The Castle, The Loco, The Vic,
I remember The *Crowie* with its landlord named Mick
I remember The Magna, The Cremorne, and The *Stute*,
I remember going in town in my *whistle and flute*.
I remember The Bowling Green, The Rifleman, The ferry,
If we had half in them all, we'd be more than merry.
I remember Scotch Mac, and his barmaid named Sue,
But I just can't remember, *One Lamp Lou*.

The heart of our meadows was about one hundred yards long
You could do all your shopping, you couldn't go wrong.
There was Boots, there was Simmons, there was Battersbys too.
There was Wilfords the Butchers, *yes* always a queue.

There was Astles the Greengrocer, not forgetting Frank Gill,
If you cold eat fruit forever, you'd get more than your fill.
There was Marsdens, Meadow Dairy, a Bendix as well,
There was even a dry cleaners run by a woman named Nell.
We didn't go in town, we didn't have to,
The only thing that was missing, I think, was a zoo.
4d on a Saturday, would take us to the *flicks*,
Superman, Batman, way after Tom Mix,
The goodies, the baddies, we'd cheer and we'd boo,
But I still can't remember *One Lamp Lou*.

There was The Castle, The Arboretum, the Embankment, The Trent,
I think nearly everyone from Nottingham went.
We had day trips to Clifton Woods and spent hours in the square,
And for three days in October, there was the Goose Fair.
Times have changed since those days, and it seems quite sad.
We didn't have a lot, but we'd share what we had.
But now the people have left and the houses have gone.
If that's what they call *progress*, I'd sooner have none.
People aren't as friendly in this day and age,
They're all too busy trying to earn a wage,
Why can't there be *characters*, we only need one or two,
Why can't there be people like *One Lamp Lou*.
Paul J Nabi

The Secret is Out
I first saw you, when you were down,
And depression filled your mind;
Then one day later you realised,
That a special love you'd find;
You found that love inside yourself,
Then wanted me to know,
But you kept it secret for awhile,
For your heart had told you so.

Then not too long your anguish showed,
When I looked into your eyes;
Your secret was out, I knew just then,
For I heard your loving cries;
The sound came deep from within your soul,
And it fell on the stars above;
'Cause that was the day, that I told you,
I too fell deep in love;

There's only one thing left to say,
And that is plain to see;
Because you are so beautiful,
I'll never set you free;
Even though our problems seem a lot,
Our love will see us through;
And knowing we're perfect in our love,
It's enough for me and you.
John D Mark

Things Happen to Me!

The door is open. I walk through
The sleeve of my overall catches too,
The handle sticking out too far,
Jogs my elbow with a jar,
Knocks out of my hand, my cup of tea
Down on the carpet, - things happen to me!

Reaching in the fridge next day
From the shelf hurtles mustard jar
Onto the floor, and breaks the lid,
And spills the mustard -
Well, I never did!
Things just happen to this kid!

An enquiring mind have I -
And three long shelves well filled
With books, but many times I wonder why
The answers aren't revealed -
To the questions bothering me -
Why do these things happen to me?
Kate Fell

Sarajevo Child
When God made the world he made it as one.
He didn't make it in bits nor create any guns.
No. Man has done that over the years,
Making divisions, creating fears,
No longer knowing how to live with each other
No longer believing each man is his brother.
Learning to hate instead of love
As into the battle the innocent we shove.
Sarajevo child, where is your arm?
What did you do to come to such harm?
And you, little girl, where is your leg?
How did you lose it? Tell me, I beg.
And little baby bathing in bath of blood
How did you get involved with this madman's flood?
This flood of hate and national pride
Where in this chaos can the innocent hide?
The innocent victims of politics' games.
Oh men of war, where is your shame?
How can you stand there and look me in the eye
When all around you the children die?

Joy Rowland

No Time

No time to weep
No time to look back
No time to stand still
No money on the window sill.

No dreams can hold me back
No scrapbook to look back on
Of things that were or might have been.

No life style, treasures, gains or regrets
No lighted fires, no diary to scan the passing years,
out of sight, out of mind.
No insight left to guide the way
another crime, another shot to pass the day.
No longing left, no footpaths to tread
Suspended in this awful dread.
Liz Dicken

All Souls No Saints?

*(In memory of the seven who lost their lives on November 30th 1993,
at the House of the Rising Sun, Greysteel)*

Trick our treat came early
to the house of the rising sun,
Is this your idea of fun?
the gun
No place to run
Maddogs poised
deafening noise,
political task
from behind the mask
blood beer sorrow and tear,
Victims,
prisoners of solitude and fear,

77

Wherefore we praised our dead
Which are already dead
more than the living
Which are yet alive,
Yea better is he than both they,
Which hath not been, who hath not seen
The evil work that is done,
Within the house
of the rising sun.
Raymond Dinsmore

Untitled

A child so small, so innocent
Who looks at the world in wonderment
has yet to discover the pain and the sorrow
of yesteryears and the dawn of tomorrow.
For looking back there is no joy
save for the love of one small boy.
Though in her eyes he walked so tall.
He knew and cared so much,
His faultless ways and tender heart
no-one, nor she, could ever touch
For he too, knew too much to tell
of his loveless life, a living hell.
Not for him the loving embrace
of arms that protect and console.
Not for him the love and the warmth
of a homely, motherly soul.
Orphans of the storm perhaps?
or kindred spirits true.
It's taken twenty years hence
to bring me back to you.
Memories of a life untold
began so painfully to unfold,
No teddy bear, no hand to hold
I felt alone and oh so cold.

I wish that you were here with me
to hold me oh so tenderly
For my love for you was pure and true
a friendship so sincere.
I wish that you were here with me
to hold me oh so near.
K Gordon

A Pray Time
Dear Lord,
Help us to over come the daily things that
come our way,
Help us to overcome nerves and to feel your presence
with us.
We thank you for giving us this day and we enjoy it to
the upmost in our hearts give us travelling mercies
wherever we may go,
And to know that you are always by our side,
You are our friend, sister, and brother and we
should love you always,
Thank you for giving us our lives and people to meet,
We can give nothing to you,
Only thank you for what you have done all we can say
That we love you always,
You are our God and master.
Doreen Whall

Nightmare of Hypothesis
Reality is one big dream
Compared to the nightmare of hypothesis.
From east to west
The sun rises, the sun sets.
Everyday a certainty
In terms of empirical infallibility.
What if observation faltered
As experience became refuted?

79

Darkness substitutes illuminating glow,
If the sun fails to rise tomorrow.
The world unable to revolve,
Shudders to a halt.
Every life form shrivels and dies.
Earth itself shrinks to a minute size.
Then we could no longer be perceived
Because there would be no one with eyes to see.
Soman Balan

Life in Exile

Oh! That I'll return some day
To the land that was my birth,
To the little cottage in the hills
No lovelier place on earth,
To leave behind these concrete towers,
The alien noise of city streets,
And go back to the simple life
To find tranquillity and peace.

And yet, if I just close my eyes
I imagine I'm still there,
Outside my little cottage
Breathing sweet, fresh mountain air,
I look out across Llyn Padarn
As the water ripples by,
And Dolbardarn Castle on the hill
Forever keeps a watchful eye.

I roam the heather covered slopes
Whilst buzzards swoop and soar,
And gaze at rugged, rocky peaks
With something close to awe
And if I'm granted one last wish
In God's almighty plan,
I'll see the sun set o'er Yr Wyddfa
And die a happy man.
Frances Jones

Hiraeth (a Song for Welsh Expatriates)

To the wild and windy moorlands
Where the soaring skylarks glide,
To the springy, reedy peat, where
Purple wimberries shyly hide;
To the mountains green and ancient,
Clothed and carpeted in pine,
Where the air is pure and fragrant
And intoxicates like wine:
       - Oh Lord, guide my errant footsteps.

To the chuckling brooks and rivers,
Quiet lakes and waterfalls,
Let me see the rainbows rising
AS the willow shades grow tall.
To the gentle rain of springtime
Bringing tides of daffodils,
Like a drift of golden sunlight
Warming meadows, woods and hills:
       - Oh Lord, guide my errant footsteps.

To the fifty-thousand voices
Stirring every Celtic heart,
Let me join that mighty chorus
When they sing *How Great Thou Art*.
To that welcome in the hillsides,
To that welcome in the vales,
To that fountain-head of hiraeth,
To my home - my home in Wales:
       - Oh Lord, guide my errant footsteps.

By the flags that bind the nation,
By the fiery dragons' tails,
So I pledge I'll never wander
When I go back home to Wales.
R Evans

The Heart of Essex

Sea breezes, scudding clouds, salt marsh,
Your soft and gentle hills, not harsh,
Those sandy cliffs, and shingle beaches rushed upon by waves,
Which in times past invaders carried to your shores.
Perhaps they brought you order, art, or other country lores.

How wild your coastal wetlands, and dusty gorse clad heath,
And wide your clear blue skydome, chequered fields beneath.
Surrounding cool green woodland, birdsong, leafy glades,
Quiet your scattered villages, and warm your country towns,
Like Finchingfield and Dunmow, roofed in golden browns.

Slow and gentle rivers, dividing Halstead, neat,
Meandering through Chelmsford, or crossing Witham Street,
Fine churches everlasting, from yew clad churchyards gaze,
And Colchester, oh Colchester, your ancient roman walls
Guard secrets of a glorious past, and modern shopping malls.

Brave the folk of Essex, who for their country fought,
Their sacrifice, for ever, in history's noose is caught.
True to the Essex homeland, guarded all their days,
At Ashingdon and Maldon, on many thorn ringed mound,
Our ancestors loved Essex with a courage rarely found.
G Wells

A Curlew's Cry

Hearing a distant curlew's bubbling cry
My heart with hiraeth fills.
This sad, lonely sound distils
Sun and wind on Wales' hills.
Michael Tod

Purley Then and Now

Purley!
Once we sat round the fountain
on warm summer evenings
watching the world go by.
Ah me!

Now it's Tesco's, traffic jams,
green men flashing
at traffic lights.
Building societies-
insurance offices - banks
charity shops in ranks-
more charity shops - and banks.

We shopped at Woolworths
Gilmores-Swattons.
The cafe where the Polish man
served dinner for half a crown
or a few shillings gave us
a trip up to town.
Ah me!

Carols at Christmas
lights in the tree
where the waterworks stood
before Tesco's.
Ah me!

Purley!
Once a small Surrey town,
a benign London outpost-
Now, just a huge supermarket -
on the way to the coast.

Ah me!
Maisie Dance

Imagine

Imagine a moon
Shining so bright
Imagine us
Kissing goodnight,
Imagine me
Holding your hand
Imagine a solid
Gold wedding band,
Imagine me
Saying hello
Imagine you
Wanting to know.
Colin Cross

Imagine If . . .

Imagine if you could keep your youth,
Would it mean you fear wisdom and truth.
Imagine if it was the end of your time,
Would those wasted moments have been your crime.
Imagine if you could read any mind,
Would you be happy with what you'd find.
Paul Corrigan

Armistice Day

No one blew a trumpet
No one banged a drum
No one told the peasants
the war had just begun.

A belly full of hunger
A heart full of tears
No one told the peasants
that this war would last for years.

Someone lost a father
Someone lost a son
No one quite remembers
when the plough turned to a gun.

Now the peasants do the killing
Their faces marked and pained
The women do the crying
their children getting maimed.

The slaughter was remorseless
With mortar and the gun
No one quite remembers
how this bloody war begun.

Now fields lie strangely quiet
With the battle won and lost
The businessman looks richer
but the peasant counts the cost.
Dave P Reddick

Remember

Remember they died for you and I
Remember the men who ruled the sky
Remember the Navy and rolling waves
Remember the soldiers on parade
Remember those who fought and died
Remember them with pride
Remember the battles of sea air and land
Remember those living who fought for their land.
Edward Barber

War

War is frightening, and viciously bloody
Cold, rainy and usually muddy,
It brings both pain and sorrow
God knows if we will see tomorrow.
Death and pain that is so sharp
They both tend to leave their mark,
If they use the bomb it is plain
There will never be war again.

Why is the world in this terrible state
Full of evil, jealousy and hate
Let us pray to God in heaven above
To fill our hearts with peace and love,
Put peace in our hearts and sense in our heads
Let us die of old age at home in our beds
Make contentment spread over us all
And little children can grow whole and tall,
Take the fear from their young lives
Let new hope appear in their eyes
This is what God intended right from the start
So I pray to the world, let peace fill your heart.
Patricia Maynard

I Wonder Why

I wonder why there's so much strife
In this old world of ours
When there's the sun, the birds, the trees
And all God's lovely flowers.

I wonder why we plan to kill
And hurt each other so
There are so many better things
To do on earth, I know.

A cheerful look, a helping hand
To aid one on the way
Would make our lives worth living
And enrich each passing day.

If only men would scheme to help
The needy and the ill -
If all the countries would unite
To strive for sheer goodwill.

What a happy place this world would be
For you and me to live in -
Instead of *taking* from each other -
Let's try a little *giving*.

Our time on earth is very short,
The years so soon pass by -
Why can't we live in peace on earth -
I wonder why?
Irene Alder

The World Outside
The world it changes everyday
No two days are the same
In some foreign countries
There are people who're in pain
Dying of starvation.
As they've got no food to eat
If only we could help them
To get back on their feet
Then there's war and hatred
Many people getting hurt
Bombs dropping everyday
Homes getting burnt,
We really don't appreciate
How lucky we may be

Having food to eat each day
A home and family
We should take each day as it comes
And hope for peace to come
And then we could live happily
Until our day is done.
Ann-Marie Lewis

Christmas

Christmas is not what it seems.
Has it lost some of what it means?
Has it been commercialised.
So we forget the birth of Christ?
People see the tinsel and the light.
But not the malevolence; not their plight.
What is this world coming to?
It is rotten right over and through
Help this world and heal it, in this day and age
Let's turn over a brand new page.
Stop the shooting.
Stop the polluting.
Clear the way for the new little child,
Stop the stupidity and stop running wild.
Planet Earth is our place,
We cannot live in outer space.
Children suffer at Christmas time
Because adults are at war all the time
A world full of hunger and homelessness
Is this the image of world Christmas?
Stop the carnage.
Stop the pillage.
Stop bombing the Bosnian village.
It's Christmas! The birthday of Christ.
Stop fighting for once in your life.
This Christmas don't let the children suffer,
Let them play hand in hand with one another.
Mark Lewis

By the Sea

Oh I do like to be beside the seaside
With its effluence and muck
Find old excreta
Really is a bit of luck!
The bottles, the baggages and the rags
To name but three
Are full of mystery and wonder
For those beside the sea.
Discovering their origins
Their contents, their insides
Will test the mental talents
Of the highly qualified
The earnest paddler peering
Detecting what is there
Lurking in the murky pools
No fish I do declare
But bits of everlasting plastic
And left off underwear
The froth of disgorged chemicals
Mingles innocuously
With the wrappings of a sarney
Disposed of carelessly.
If you should pause and ponder
I'm sure you will agree
The world is full of wonder
And excitement by the sea.
Alice Peterson

This Desperate City is Immortal

In this desperate city which is immortal
the hounds of the pearl eyed secrets
stir upon the razored steps of night.
The evening then, descends as gold dust.

89

You all who now walk with me of new
I see in you the ghost of love
from last winter's leap, leap into streets
where this silent brood can no longer tread
for I am crippled with the madness of this city
which is immortal.

In the multitude of the solitude
I saw and caught your rumba glance
and we danced through the grey streaky cloud
of childhoods from afar and perhaps
beneath a London star you were my first kiss
of love and you are of gold dust.
In this desperate city which is immortal.
Olly Rees

Dreamland

Born and bred in London, I was a city girl
Among its noisy bustle, fog and traffic swirl.
Oft' I dreamed of the country where the air was fresh and clean
And places I only visited, when I was young and green.

I was nineteen when it happened, the anticipated curse
Of war descended upon us, while I trained as a nurse.
Homes were reduced to rubble when bombs rained from above
And moonlit nights were a menace, instead of a mood for love.

I felt the heat of the fires, saw Spitfires pirouette in the air
And when war was finally over, I danced in Trafalgar Square!
Painful memories faded, such is the way of life,
Along with childish fancies when I became a wife.

The years added up to retirement, suddenly free to leave
And find a home in the country where the air is fit to breathe.
Scarce arrived in Monkton, a cacophony blasted us all
As the hurricane's exhalations caused many a tree to fall.

Though shaken by disaster, everyone did their best
To see more trees were planted and keep the county dressed.
Now, I look from my window to see ponies grazing there;
Sometimes, sheep or cattle - and birds are everywhere.

Just down the road - the sea! No longer *as a moat*
So I'll not use the Tunnel, I'll visit France by boat.
I'd rather feel the sun or sea breeze in my hair
Than be prematurely buried in the underground, down there!

London has its pleasures for those who seek a crowd
But people here are kinder, where greeting is allowed.
So I breathe a prayer of thanks for every moment spent
In the place I used to dream about - the beautiful County of Kent.
C E Bradford

London

Dignified stature forms the pulse of a land
Rising beside murky waters.
An awe of majesty overwhelms
In this untiring place
Rhythms of life abound.

Men in suits behind bustling walls
Finance, the Arts, Political brawls
A body of nobles and business moguls.
Statues peering upon crowded squares
Pushing and shoving, selling of wares.

Beneath flows a network
The school of commuters
In retail, banking, computers
Silenced by the stigma of British restraint
A stampede of humility squeezing through gates.

A royal location of splendour and pearls
An abundance of riches, shared with the world.
Yet in the streets that are paved with gold
Lay the beds of its people hungry and cold
Huddled in shadows of depravation
As the big clock chimes the hour of a nation.

Here a centre not heaven or hell
Where homelessness neighbours
High fashion and wealth
No rich hand saves a beggar's pity
Though a passion is shared for their great city.
Paula C Graham

Our Land of Wales
Wales is a land of castles and views
Of lamb and cockles and delicious stews
Wales is a land of Choirs and Coal
Of people who laugh with their men on the dole.
Wales is a land of tips and waste.
Where owners grabbed their profits and left in haste
Where pit head gears lie idle and die with rust
Where old miners gasp and cough up dust.
But Wales is a land in spite of it all
Goes mad with joy with a rugby ball.
The singing in the *Arms Park* is strong and loud.
Fifteen *Taffies* feel so proud.
They remember they are *Cymro's*
With hearts so full of pride
They play to win and never give in
With all that *Hwyl* inside
They remember their forefathers
Who fought in Hills and Dales
And left us our inheritance
This lovely land called Wales.
Doug Stephens

Untitled

As I awake each morning
And behold the sky
What inner joy it gives
As the day goes by.

The glorious golden sun
As it rises in the sky
Casting its wonderful golden light
Over the earth and sky.

The ever changing scenes
As the clouds float by
Revealing the wonderful
Blue of the sky.

And the occasions when I see
A rainbow in the sky,
I am forever grateful to
Look up to behold the sky.
June Misson

The Secret Garden

Locked in a private world, of fears and self-contempt,
Where the seeds of doubt, grow into buds of resent.
Parasitic tendrils, creep out from a central core,
Single-minded in purpose, intent on all to devour.

The weeds of self-pity, once rooted, are hard to move,
Channelling their efforts into one, ever-deepening, grove.
Any attempt to break the stem, a futile waste of time,
For the root that's left behind can reform, and redesign.

These happenings in a garden, behind a very high wall,
Any attempts at which to scale, could end in a fatal fall.
This very secret garden, in the midst of a dense wood,
Impervious to all, but the most insistent flood.

93

The trees, all packed together, only the tiniest gap between,
Ensure fragmented glimpses, are all that can be seen.
To a passing traveller, the wood, indeed, looks grim,
If only he would make a path, let healthy light in.

Occasional passing travellers, pause, then are on their way,
If only one would decide, for a while, at least, to stay.
For deep within that garden, are flowers waiting to grow,
To shyly unfold their petals, and capture the sun's glow.

But whilst the weeds surround them, and the parasite threads
                                                    its way,
Those flowers cannot grow, so buried they must stay,
The trees need to be thinned, a gate made in the wall,
Weeds and parasites destroyed, so the flowers can make their call.

Then other passing travellers will pause, and maybe stay,
To bask in the garden, watch the dance of the sun's ray.
From flower to flower it passes, showing each in its best light,
Each, a vision of splendour, to enchant and delight.
E M Walker

My Garden

I bought a house with garden too.
I thought of renovating it as people do
After the house the garden I think.
I'll make it shipshape and in the pink.
A pond came quickly to my mind
With fish and lilies of a kind.
Also a net to stop the cats.
From pawing out the little sprats,
All this in picture I could see,
So I set about it, to please me,
I started a hole the shape of a heart
Well I thought it is a start.

The rubbish I found it came to pass.
I found the soil all full of glass.
A sieve I thought is what I need
So down I got upon my knees
The glass just twinkled laying there
Giving me thought to be aware
Cardboard boxes soon got full
With twinkling glass and rubbish too,
The fish pond soon came into shape
Into the hole I could only gape
Three foot four foot that would be fine
Anyone would I was digging a mine.
The plastic pond of coloured hue
Wouldn't fit as I wanted too.
A little pat here a little pat there
Just about sent me to despair,
After a while it fell into place
So I pegged it there just in case.
D J Hilton

Time is Winding Up

Engrossed in worldly affairs?
Look deeper immortal man.
Examine, rethink, destroy me not.
The offer, escape from the plastic dustbin.
Retreat with me says nature
With its constant guileful smile
For I will lead you to the maker of all things.
Take heed of my awesome stare.
Colin Howard

We Could Save the Planet

Why is there always talk of growth?
It is the western politician's oath.
No, the talk should be of living within our means,
And the human race must limit passing on its genes.

Our planet is fragile, finite and rare,
We must it with all God's creatures share.
But we take too much and give little back.
Big business contributes much to this lack.
We must consider these things before it's too late,
We are all answerable for our planet's fate.
Wendy Rowland

A Legacy to our Descendants

There's a move afoot to cover the country with new roads.
Sustainable development, to carry lots of loads,
To and from the Tunnel, new business to inspire:
Create new jobs, employment, and wealth we should desire.

New Business Parks, and industry, the Councils have the Plan.
It's called Strategic Guidance, they're for it to a man.

Hang on a sec; how long did it take to grow those ancient trees?
Will replanting help the feeling of belonging, if you please?

To see green fields all covered up and in their place, great lorries,
With noise and fumes, the wildlife gone; it's causing us great worries.

The councils' smug, developers hug the prospect of great profit.
Will Conscience vow, in years from now, 'twas only for your benefit.
Jean Hopkinson

The Executive

He was destined to go far
With prospects and a company car
Long before the recession came
Bringing redundancy and shame,
Now his life seems nil, and void
Part of Britain's unemployed

96

Chasing vacancies where the plan
Is to employ a younger man
So he thinks is there no work for me
Can I be too old at forty three.
Margaret Thompson

Blame

What do you think when you see what wars do?
Do to a nation of mixed peoples and races
What do you feel when you see their faces?
Pity . . . compassion. But who is to blame, who?

Nations divided -
Friend against friend -
Will their relationships ever be mend?
Who gets the blame, have you decided?

Is it leaders or followers, who gets the blame?
Or us who watch and feel but ignore it
Convincing ourselves we loathe and abhor it
After all it's not us, why should we worry?

But, how will we ever have peace if we never
Find who's to blame for those of our future . . .
Forever.
Jill McIlveen

The Six O'Clock News

When I watch telly while eating my tea
lies and murder is all I can see.
Somebody's dead, a bullet can kill
but no I am not watching The Bill.

A little boy, he's at play,
a kidnapper is on the way,
grabs the boy and runs away.
But, Eastenders is not on today.

A teenage girl walks down a street
Not knowing the danger she's going to meet.
Along a dark alley a man awaits
he's going to steal the young girl's fate.

Along a dark street, there's a parked car,
a teenage boy walks out of a bar.
A family's grieving the loss of a son.
That young drunken driver was doing a ton.

A group of young kids are out on a rave
One of those kids ends up in her grave.
Nobody told her the dangers of drugs
Now her mum is missing her hugs.

While I am sitting here eating my peas
A young copper falls down to his knees.
There were no witnesses or any clues
Yes, I am watching the six o'clock news.
G Saunders

Trouble Spots

It's not right, it's not fair
Sending our boys over there.
Why should they get involved?
It won't help to get things solved.
They have to go, have no say,
They don't even get any extra pay.
Left behind are the kids and wives
To get on, alone, with their lives.
Worrying, are our men safe and well?
Back home we're going through hell.

98

We see it all on the news,
Hearing all the different views.
It's our boys' safety we care about -
About that there can be no doubt.
So hurry home, when your jobs are done,
We're waiting for you, to have some fun.
You'll deserve lots of tender loving care,
After six lonely months over there.
And here we are, to give it to you,
Your precious families, faithful and true.
Gill Sumner

The Day of Glory

I remembered the posters, the songs they would sing -
Those encouraging words of song -
I remembered the glory they said war would bring,
As the battle slowly raged on.

I tried to think through the shout to *Advance*,
As the enemy ran for cover.
But now, it seems, I am given my chance
For the battle is all over.

I look at the field of numberless dead,
And think to myself, 'How?'
Tales of grandeur filled my head,
But where's the glory now?

I must be a hero now, I guess,
As our side won the day.
Most of my friends lie dead in this mess,
And there's nothing left to say.

The people of London, hearing of this,
Will give themselves three cheers,
Saying, 'Wish I was there,' and airing their views
And they will shed no tears.

99

They cannot know what is happening here,
Of all this sorrow and strife,
They cannot know this incessant fear
That I live but to lose my life.

These are my thoughts as I look at this place
Where ten thousand, it seems have died.
This is the truth which I cannot face,
So behind the glory I'll hide.
Jennifer E Pocock

Deeds From Dreams
With you I will share everything -
My knowledge and my sadness.
You want to hold me and kiss
My face as I sleep. Although I've
Yet to find you I love you.
I have to.
Robert James Carr

Oh I Hate Being Skinny
Imagine if I wasn't skinny,
With my ribs sticking out,
I'd love to be portly,
Rotund and very stout.

Instead of legs like matchsticks,
I'd have legs like huge tree-trunks,
Big muscles like a wrestler,
And flesh you could cut in chunks.

I'd never have to be afraid,
Of walking over a drain,
In case I should suddenly fall in,
Never to seen again.

But, I've me brighter moments,
Me bits of harmless fun,
Like going to *Weight-Watchers*,
When a session's going on!
Ian Christopher

Imagine If

Imagine if ten pound notes were butterflies
And bees were gold to match them,
Would not people run around
And wouldn't people catch them.

Imagine chocolate bars were golden nuggets
And ices were gold to match,
Would not people chase about,
And wouldn't them people catch.

Imagine if jellies were very large rubies
And champagne red just like them,
Would not one want them to eat
Also to drink, enjoy them.

Imagine now if a ring a ring of roses
Were put into a teapot,
What would come out of the spout
A cup of tea like red wine.

Imagine if a ship was passing in the night
Saw a lady in the sea,
And she was turning the ship
Tipping it in the ocean.

Imagine if trees and leaves were a brilliant red
And the sky the same colour,
Would not people run away
And wouldn't people follow!

Imagine if the blue sea was like a sapphire
And the pebbles to match them,
Would not people rush around
And would not people bank them!
Gwen Albon

Imaginary World
Imagine if there was no pain,
No sickness or despair
Imagine if the blind could see,
The mute could speak, the deaf could hear.

Imagine if there was no war
No murder, rape or crime,
This world would be a better place
In which to spend our time.

Imagine if there was no news
Of evil far and wide
And only good news to report
Love in man's heart abide.

We'd all go 'round with smiling face
The sun would always shine,
My goods and chattels I would share
With neighbour, friend, what's mine is thine.

Alas! 'Tis only but a dream
In my imagination
As only God could bring about
This perfect new creation.
Jean Carroll

A Double Life

I use my imagination to give my life a double meaning,
The first in the day the second when I'm dreaming.
My imagination is an escape from harsh reality,
A way of forgetting true brutality.
In real life I'm all alone,
People rarely visit my home.
When they do they only mock me,
My imagination sets me free.
I dream I have love and friends,
By using my imagination my broken heart mends.
My second life is full of laughter and fun,
Joy and pleasures brought to me by everyone.
No more emptiness and no more tears.
My imagination has helped me to survive all these years,
Because in real life I am lonely and blue,
But with my imagination I can try to make my dreams come true.
Andrea Jane Blue

Eighteen Months Old

Once lying helpless in my arms,
Bewildered by all that's around,
Glancing, focusing on my face,
Suckling away hunger with gentle grace.

From sitting to crawling to standing, to walking
From milk to finger foods I have watched you eating.
From gurgles to babbles, to mama, to dada
No longer a baby and only just a toddler.

You stand at the mirror,
Grinning as wide as can be.
You pull lots of faces,
To explore the new me.

103

Pointing your finger
You shout out No!
You practice like an actress
For a part in a TV show.

The bricks are a cake,
You are busy making tea
Doll doll you have rocked to sleep
And thrown on the settee.

The play dough is for eating,
The yoghurts finger paint,
The dish is a hat,
And why should you go to bed?
It's not very late.

You bounce and dance and try to sing
You amuse us day after day
With the joy that you bring.

Watching you sleeping in the still of the night
I feel my heart jump with sheer delight.
Sandra Coulter-Ellis

Clouds

On warm days in the summer
When the sun rides high
I lie down on the scented grass
And watch the clouds drift by.

I ponder where they come from
Or where they are going to go.
Or on the things they chance to meet
Like rain or hail or snow.

Some clouds I am sure are friendly,
They are so fluffy and so white,
While other clouds look menacing
As dark as dark as night.

Some clouds seem so gentle
As they ride upon the breeze,
Yet others simply push and shove
And do just as they please.

Then storm clouds bring a change of scene
To the friendly sky.
With anger and with venom,
They lash all from up high.

But soon the sun rides out again,
And smiles to all below,
It seems to say no rain today.
I am sure it really knows.

So I lie upon the grass again,
And stretch out peacefully,
It's wonderful to watch the clouds
Drift high up over me.
Victor J Pike

Tree
Tree, old and wise,
Tree, in leaf disguise;
Tree, deep roots hold,
Tree, damp moss cold;
Tree, chaffinch on bough,
Tree, climbing infants row;
Tree, gnarled and eerie,
Tree, shades traveller weary,

Tree, sweet blossom fair,
Tree, grey squirrel lair;
Tree, man and saw,
Tree, alas, no more.
Paul Lilley

Promise of Spring
The leaves flutter down
Making carpets of gold
And there's a chill in the air
As winter starts to unfold.

The heavy dew glistens
In the early morning hours,
Like beads of silver, rests on cobwebs
And what's left of the flowers.

The weak sun breaks through the cloudy sky
And the now leafless trees break its ray.
Casting frail shadows upon the ground,
In a vain attempt to warm the day.

A robin hops by -
Searching for food on its way
Its bright red breast
Brightens up the dull day.

The first flakes of snow
Have started to fall.
Pretty soon there will be
No colour at all.

Yes, winter's arrived
With all it may bring.
Fog, rain, ice and snow,
But, the promise of spring.
Janet Endersby

Nature's Ways

The winter coat of white
replaces golden colours of autumn,
icy finger tips, touches and caresses
and lingers, tracing patterns with ever changing ways.

Days so cold and frosty nights
trees bare all, yet show nothing,
nature sends messages, then comes response
the slow drip of water, as the thaw sets in.

The bite of the wind
loosens its hold and retreats,
oh so slowly licks its wounds
stinging from sudden withdrawal.

As the warmth of the sun
sends shivers of delight,
and the coldness prepares for
the ultimate glowing warmth.

At last the colour green
responds to a gentle nudge,
and reaches out tormenting it
into forming new buds of growth.

This heralds the return of spring
and freshness appears once again,
forcing its strength to release
life to the forefront.

Days fermenting into weeks
and months of sparkling enjoyment,
never ceasing and never ending
seasoned with nature's ways.
John Whitwell

Autumn Leaves

Autumn leaves are falling
Yet never make a sound
Falling down so softly
Until they reach the ground,
They look quite nice and colourful
In shades of golden browns
But the leaves have their comebacks
As they nestle to the ground.
Everywhere you look you see
Them scattered all around,
Trees now are looking quite bare
From all leaves they have shed
As you walk amongst the leaves
You hear them rustle beneath your tread.
Margaret Rose Marsh

Winter Seascape

Clouds drifting over
The deserted beach,
Only the tiniest,
Footprint,
Tells the story.
I don't want to go home
To tea.
The last tripper gone,
The sea
Puts on her
Winter mantle
And like Grandma,
Falls gracefully
To sleep.
Carole Smith

108

The Tree

Its peacefulness is overwhelming,
With posture so unique
and blossom like hair in the wind.
It's every colour of the rainbow
and a friend to all creation.
We are the trees' breath and the tree is ours
but man is determined it must die
for trivial products for you and I.
It's crushed hacked and set alight
with its screams heard by those who want to.
Its blood now black dust over desolate land.
Cures for the sick have now vanished
and the beauty of this once majestic being.
We need to stop the destruction
as soon, we will be where the tree lies
because without it, we will also die.
Donna Payne

I Am the Golden Eagle

The ultimate symbol
of strength and pride
is soaring with eagles in the sky
so I could see things from a different view
not just me, so could you.
I could see rivers, trees and nature as it really is
the soaring symbol of enduring strength
landing far away on some person's fence.
Some eagles may be old,
but I'll tell you this,
they've got wings of gold.
I who trust in the Lord will find my strength
renewed and will rise on wings like an eagle.

I woke up one day
and thought I could fly
as high as an eagle in the sky.
I will soar on my mighty wings
to far away places
seeing what this life could really bring.

Lee Mitchelson

Through the Trees

The wondrous flight of birds
The constant work of bees.
But how seldom heard
The magnificence of trees.
Straight as a die, supple as babes,
Reaching great heights if man behaves.

The ash, alder, aspen and beach,
All within our easy reach.
On deep chalky soils, during a walk
Here to one hundred feet, observe the beech.
Poplar, rowan, elm and maple,
To these shore all long staple.

Chestnut, larch, lime and more,
Birch, spruce, fir and sycamore.
Sturdy oak, supple willow, graceful pine,
All for centuries have grown fine.
Tall ones, short ones, varied and plenty,
Different species, at least twenty.

Of famous ships old sailors once spoke,
'Their hulls' they gleamed *of solid oak*.
Their longboats designed to dash,
Pulled by oars of straight ash.
And weapons made mainly from wood,
Protected our forefathers when firmly they stood.

110

For hundreds of years trees may live,
If man and disease do not blight.
Their branches offering shade and shelter,
With a high pitched song on a windy night.
Sometimes a ghostly appearance on frosty dawns,
But, their majestic beauty a never ending delight.
H Smith

Late at Plough
The tractor's blue, stuttering fume,
and a foaming wake of gulls all day,
until the light leadens along the hill,
and the rooks stream steadily away.

While overhead, the lapwings loom like leafy trees,
dusk smudges out the last, long line of the sun
where it touches the turned, dark land:
and a star comes, like a benediction.
Jim Hodson

Sunset
The sun it sets,
behind the wheat,
while here upon,
the grass I seat,
as if the world has finally ended,
from silence into peace.

Here on earth,
revenge we seek,
to flatten the land,
with concrete feet,
can this land,
beyond concrete,
keep its beauty so discreet,
or is this land past defeat.
Matthew Longfoot

Graceful Waters

The waters reflect gently in the sun
flickering rippling in the smooth flow
I could stay here all day just dreaming into the graceful pond.
> And the ducks glide by
> And the ducks glide by
> And the ducks laugh are they laughing at me.

I lay my head back on the old pond bench
to see jet planes fly so high and as quiet and as small
as a pin prick carving a white line through the sky
like a knife.
> And the ducks glide by
> And the ducks glide by
> And the ducks laugh are they laughing at me.

David Genney

The Leaves on the Trees

The leaves on the trees
fall gently to the ground
and sparkling frost
shines all around
and snowdrops suddenly appear.
It's plain to see that
winter's here
and when things 'round us
get so bad
we're sad, and yet
we're also glad
to know dear Lord
that thou art near,
and soon midst clouds
you will appear
to make this earth
a better place
and bring peace and love
to the human race.

Brian Wood

November

Soft smoky clouds, like floating plumes of grey
Drift aimlessly across the quiet sky,
And merge into its dimness far away.
Muffing the lonely seabird's distant cry.

A band of limpid blue, like mountain stream,
Steals silently between the drifting clouds
And on the glistening sand, with paler gleam,
Mirrors its sadness, wrapped in evening's shrouds.

A wreathing fringe of seabirds undulates
Across the scene, and disappears from sight.
In solitary grief, all nature waits
Till spring shall come again in glowing light.
J Brunskill

The Birds

Winter time, the trees are bare
With branches tinged with frost
Our summer birds have flown away
Over the seas they've crossed,
We miss them chirping in the trees
How we long for spring
Then suddenly it has arrived
Oh it's a wondrous thing.
And with it our birds back again
After miles of flight
Singing their sweet songs of life
They are a lovely sight
So feed our birds take care of them
Because I must confess
These birds give something back to me
It's one word. Happiness.
Barbara Fleming

Old Age

Growing old is another phase of life
But never think it's the end of strife
Do not imagine your problems all cease
Or you'll know what it's like to have perfect peace.

Unless you had a position previous where you could save cash
In retirement you can't do anything rash,
You rely on state pension that really is low my friend,
But the bills never shrink or never end.

Your hearing gets worse and your bones start to creak
Youngsters look at you odd if to them you speak
Your hair turns white if you've any left on your head
And it takes great effort to get out of bed.

But it's not all bad when you reach a mature age
It's like opening a new chapter reading a new page
No longer restricted in what to do or say
Not working and watching a clock every day,

Go out when you want old friends to see
Drop into a cafe for a scone and some tea
You've got this far enjoy the beauty still around
Don't despair, or give in pleasures are still to be found.
A Cane

The Challenge

Kath's into training
For a bike ride
Just to be a comfort
At her husband's side.
Land's End to John O' Groats
That is their aim
Pushing on the pedals
Then doing it again

114

It's a very long way
And a gruelling test
But I know with God's help
They will do their best.
Thelma Robinson

Unspoken Words

I once had a friend not so very long ago
The best friend a person could want
She was always there when you
Had a moan with a cup of tea
And a buttered scone.
She patiently listened to all your woes
And even showed you how to sew clothes
She taught me to knit, iron and cook
And even how to read a book
She's gone now this friend
And I miss her so,
I loved her but never told her so,
I wish I had I must have been dumb,
Not to have told her
I love you mum.
Sheila Hutchinson

Mother in Law

My mother in law has got the flu
And I don't think she'll cope
As she's ninety two.
Some folks think she should live with us,
But each time she comes there's a terrible fuss.
I know we've a room - in fact we've got two,
But she can't climb the stairs, or get to our loo.
She says she's quite happy living alone,
As her bed is downstairs and her chair near the phone.

My mother in law has got the flu,
I just wish I knew what was best to do.
If she lived in a *home* the family could visit,
I think that is best and then I think *is it?*
Whether we're rich or whether we're poor
I know we all value our own front door.
Hurry up and get better dear mother in law.
Moyra Wells

The Dreamer

So calm and peaceful is the night,
As I stroll down the lane in the moonlight.
I'm going to meet Mary, I mustn't be late,
She's waiting for me by the old rustic gate.
Arms outstretched and her sweet winsome smile,
I take Mary's hand, we linger a while,
Gazing at stars shining so bright,
The moon lighting up the sky in the night.
But no twinkling star on the bluest of skies,
Can compare with my Mary's lovely eyes.
Her golden hair, her beautiful face,
So kind, so gentle, so full of grace;
Is always before me, night and day,
She'll neither fade nor go away.
We've met down the lane for many a long year,
By the gate waits my *Mary,* so patient, so dear.
Though darkness may fall she is still clearly seen,
For Mary became an angel when she was seventeen.
I never really lost her, how could we ever part?
For all through my lifetime she has lived on in my heart.
Time is drawing near Mary, when we'll be side by side,
Then I'll be young again dear, as on the day you died.
I'll meet you soon my own true love,
Not down the lane but in heaven above.

I'll stroke your hair as I did long ago,
Kiss your precious face for I love you so.
My years have now exceeded four score,
Just beckon sweetheart and I shall dream no more.
Esther Webster

Sarajevo
They did not want to die, it never was their war.
One minute they were playing
The next they were no more.
What sort of people are they, to shoot a child at play?
To watch a crumpled body fall
To never see another day.
Frightened women wait to pick up their daily bread
Food is scarce it's all they have
To keep their children fed.
Grief stricken mourners stand around a grave
Bullets flying past them as silently they pray.
What makes a man a monster
When his country is at war?
Does he put his mind on hold
When shooting at the poor
Unsuspecting innocents caught up in the bloodshed.
Does he feel remorse at all
Seeing children lying dead?
And when he is returning to his own part of the city
Marching through the ruins
Does he now feel pity?
As he sees, what other men have done
Soldiers from the other side, killing just like him.
Nobody here is winning this stupid pointless mission
The only ones who think they've won
Are the inhuman politicians.
Sylvie Cox

117

Poverty

Where is the novelty in poverty?
A penny, a pound,
Is nowhere to be found,
eyes on the street,
looking on the ground.

Can't ask him, he's too smart,
I know he'll think I'm a tart.
If only they knew the poverty trap.

Once you have been there,
there's no going back,
Money can change you,
that's what they say,
But where's the compassion for those who pray?

Position your life in reverse,
You'd think it were a curse.
I'm sure then you would expect to open your purse.

It is easily done,
Your life span has just begun,
Remember your misdeals,
Your callous ways,
You sow what you reap,
and it haunts you in your sleep.
Lisa Kennett

Lock it Up

It's amazing that some folk will enter your home
Especially if carelessly left undone
There is no end to what they will do
If they have decided to pick you.
They will browse through your things
See all that you own
Not a thing will be left alone.

Think it fun to interfere
With belongings you have and hold most dear.
Finally, things may walk out the door
Things you have treasured and a whole lot more.
Then *Lock it up* that's what I say
That you don't come off worse at the end of the day.
There are villains about in these dreadful days
To break and enter they will find ways
They always leave some tell-tale mark
That will identify them if you are sharp.
If you suspect something is wrong - lay a trap
That unsuspectingly will them nap.
Be on your guard - crime is about
Lock up your car and don't be caught out
Be more careful, you know you ought
With the Law on your side, see the culprits are caught.
'Lock it up,' again I say
And make it more difficult that they
May turn away and think better of it
And from your goods not make a profit.
Evelyn Evans

Guns in Their Hand
What words can I say to you?
What actions should I take?
Your unnecessary violence is making me ache.
Should I ignore you or deplore
You or accept my fate,
Can I trust in justice to undo your mistakes?
The pressure is hurting me I
Have to know soon,
Should I fight violence with violence or
Live on the moon?
Wherever you go,
Whatever you say
I hear our future generations breaking down.

119

Who takes the can when
Little James hits the ground
'Cos I can hear the kids
Laughing with guns in their hands.
Andrew Alison

Mugged

Without warning
I was mugged
by old age.
It crept up behind me
and put its arms around me.

I struggled
but it was no use
I was helpless in its grasp
left wondering where my energy had gone.

I tried to escape
I went to the Body Shop,
but all the decent bodies
had been taken,
by younger people.
Alistair Miller

Scourge of the Skylines

By merciful providence
And the dimension of time,
Wordsworth and Coleridge, Shelley, Keats
Belong to another age;
Even their sickened ghosts need haunt us no more.
They do not witness
Their beloved hills and skylines -
Carnmenellis, Mynydd Eppynt,
Ogden, Ovenden Moor -
Annihilated by industrial units set in tons of concrete.

Hundreds of replicas of Nelson's monument
With sails flailing to the sound of demented wasps;
Now here, now some way off,
Now absent in a time of blessed calm.
Windfarms (euphemistically named)
To power your razor and hair drier.
Even if they scrapped these monster power stations
They could never afford to remove the skeletons.
In a world of money values
Man goes progressively mad,
(And there is one thing these contraptions do generate
And that is money.)
What price a few long haired objectors
And pussyfooted local authorities
Beside vast conglomerates
More powerful than governments?
Do we wonder at vandalism,
With such examples held aloft
As if to edify?
Michael Woodhouse

Progress
Not only did fashion, change the world of dress,
The wonders of the world, have shown us progress.
Going to the moon, seemed an impossible task,
But that impossible was conquered at long last.
As oil comes rushing from the ground,
Such an abundance to be found,
Oil sheikhs are unhappy, and wear a frown,
Now we are making a few million pound.
Natural gas here, proved to be quite cheap,
Divers have been working in the North Sea deep.
The robot can work twenty four hours in a day,
He's taken over from man without any pay.

If only the Loch Ness monster can be found, ·
Who knows it may give off a really new sound.
Soon we shall journey, from England to France direct,
When the Euro Tunnel, shows off its enormous project.
If no more wars we can guarantee,
The whole wide world, will dance with glee.
C M Moody

The General's Accomplishment
What does a General say to his troops,
When he knows they are being led to their doom?
How does his conscience -
Twist and turn in the darkness?
Why does he live,
When he has achieved so much?

I have gathered this mob,
From the corners of the earth.
From every pit and cage,
Where only the vermin dwell.
Coerced, cajoled and connived,
To have them believe in a cause.
To spend their life,
On an illusion of glory.
A cause which meant . . .
Nothing to me.

Now I watch them march -
To their end, or worse,
The crushing of their fighting spirit,
Running away from fear or me.

As I contemplate my soldiers,
Who lay rotting on the pitch.
Remembering how they joked and laughed,
About war, spoken as if it were a game.
Made them believe in me.

It bothers me . . . if only for a moment,
But time has a way of masking all wounds.
In its soothing, naive embrace and in time,
While I convince others to believe in false truths,
I won't care . . .
Jassen Venkaya

A Ray of Hope

The sound of rain in chilly storm,
Each tiny drop to stir my ancient mind,
To nostalgic memories of hopes forlorn,
Must I forever seek, yet never find?
Did I possess my chosen goal?
Unaware to me, as an unseen soul
Oft' I wonder, search and pry,
The many lonely hearts that cry,
Perhaps when all the rain has gone,
A finer world we'll live upon.
Lena Tavernor

Snow

Silently falling out the sky
Snow is anything but dry
Laying a blanket that's smooth and clean
Looking at it, it's definitely not mean,
Tiny crystals soft and small
Quietly drifting down the wall
Snow is wet and white
It really is a beautiful sight
When it melts it looks like slush
Maybe even a little like mush.
Jerene R Irwin (10)

Windy City

In the windy city on Westminster Bridge
That's where thousands of the down and outs live
They do live out in the cold where the
Wind does blow out in the snow
And all, nothing to eat with often
Rags on there feet no hope at all
With their backs to the wall and
Just about two if they are lucky
Enough when Big Ben does chime two
A van comes around with
A free bowl of soup and a blanket
Or two. A fire in a bucket to
Keep themselves warm so when
You have had plenty to eat
And tucked up in bed nice
And warm and fast asleep
Do give a thought to the poor
Lonely down and outs
Who live on the streets.
With nothing to eat
And no hope at all.
So if you see a
Down and out in
The street with nothing to eat
Lend a helping hand and think to
Yourself this could be you.
Eileen Ashbridge

Elegy
(In memory of beloved husband)

Like homing birds that swiftly wheel in flight
Seeking safe haven 'ere the night steals
Slanting down the quiet eaves,
Whilst over the twilit garden weaves
A magic mystic calm in the fading light.

This was the hour he loved, his hand on the latch,
Closing the gate, sought the coveted match
For the pipe he loved, his face wreathed in contentment and peace.
From his cupped hands the flame entwindled his face,
Blue smoke encompassed him, all about!
Such a man was he, sweet and sound as a pippin,
Mellowed by autumn's sun or buffeted by its winds
Upright was he, dauntless of circumstance, unbowed
By secret griefs on his life's run he hated war, and gladly did
                                        his stint, yet full of fun.
True and beloved by all, this man of integrity!
So, like his beloved birds at the close of day,
His honeysuckle and roses passing on his way,
The tall white lilies drenched in dew,
Flowers he loved, whose scents he knew.
So day was done, and all tools laid away,
For use, by other hands, nor his, some other day,
The long shadows falling across the grass
And children's voices calling over the field;
Just quietly left, nor ever looked behind,
His valiant soul a heavenly peace to find,
Came the quiet homing of his heart at rest,
In still green pastures, with his master blest,
Joan Greathead

Kinderscout

I must go up on Kinder
That wild and rough terrain.
The joy of the climb up on Kinder
Is calling me again.

I've seen sudden changes on Kinder
With white flakes swirling 'round,
Enjoying the views I've walked
On snow and peat mottled ground.

I've sat in the sun on Kinder
The first week in November
Bilberry leaves for a cushion
These are scenes to remember.

At the Downfall up on Kinder
In wind and lashing rain,
I've crept under a rock and waited
For strength to go on again.

There are desolate places on Kinder
With peat groughs brown and bare.
You walk with silent tread
The peace is complete up there.

I want to go up on Kinder
Many times nature's blessings to share
And when my legs are too old
Memory will take me there.
Ethel M Stanton

The Stream

Intrigued! In woods I wandered,
As in a dream,
Appearing there before me,
A gentle, rippling stream,
Observing all its mystery,
It beckoned me to see,
The silver fishes diving,
In water fresh and free.
Over leaning branches,
With song birds twittering,
The sun shining brightly,
Its rays glittering,
Enticing me to follow,

Along by its side,
I came across a waterfall,
With stepping stones to stride,
Tucked in this enchanting scene,
Wild flowers it did hide,
Bluebells, Primrose, Violets,
Rabbits too, its pride!
Revealing all God's glory
My eyes open wide,
All feeling of tranquillity,
Comes over, with humility.
Muriel E Owen

Life in the 90's

Have you got a cig mate or do you have 10p?
I haven't got my cheque through and there's nowt in for tea.
Can I loan the bus fare, I'm late for my interview,
I'll pay you back on Friday when my money's through.
Don't forget to budget electric, gas and rent.
VAT and poll tax ensures your money's spent.
Give to education, give to kids in need.
Give a bit to Green Peace as the posters plead.
Spend a bit on leisure, that can do no harm
But before you set off for the pub, switch on your alarm.
Relax and put your feet up
Allow yourself sometime.
Tune into TV-AM see violence porn and crime.
Work overtime and Sundays if you value your career.
But don't get tired and don't fall ill or you're out on your ear.
And if you labour hard enough
So you're not filled with hunger,
Don't be surprised when you're told one day
Sorry, we've found someone younger.
Patricia Hepworth

The War Effort

There's a war out in the sands.
Our boys fighting in a far off land.
Photos of loved ones in a locket.
Or tucked away in a secret pocket.

Bombs and guns are everywhere
Jet-fighters buzzing in the air.
They have a cause, this they know too well.
They wish they could cast a magic spell.

If they could, it would be for peace world-wide.
Then they could be home by their loved one's side.
But in the end they'll come smiling through.
Especially with a prayer from you.
Lesley A Baldwin